A HISTORY
OF
EVERYDAY
THINGS IN
ENGLAND

BOOKS BY THE QUENNELLS

EVERYDAY THINGS IN ENGLAND

Medium 8vo.

"EVERYDAY LIFE" SERIES

Large Crown 8vo.

EVERYDAY THINGS IN GREECE

Medium 8vo.

THE GOOD NEW DAYS

A Series of bright and informative talks about the fundamental factors of British Citizenship. Fully illustrated.

Demy 8vo.   (*Out of print*)

Elizabeth Hunting

GAMES   COSTUME   SHIPS

CHURCHES

CASTLES HOUSES

COACHES

TOYS

A HISTORY
OF
EVERYDAY
THINGS IN
ENGLAND

DONE IN FOUR
VOLS., OF WHICH
THIS IS THE SECOND

1500   1799

ARMOUR   MILLS   FOOD

FOURTH
EDITION
NINTH IMPRESSION
REVISED AND ENLARGED

Written and Illustrated by
MARJORIE AND C.H.B.QUENNELL.

Published by
B.T. BATSFORD, LTD LONDON.

TO
P. C. Q.
G. E. Q.
&
R. P. Q.

P.C.Q.

First Impression . . . . October 1919
Second Impression. . . . November 1920
Third Impression, Revised . . December 1924
Fourth Impression (Second Edition) September 1930
Fifth Impression (Third Edition) October 1937
Sixth Impression . . . . July 1942
Seventh Impression . . . Winter 1944–5
Eighth Impression . . . Winter 1947–8
Ninth Impression (Fourth Edition) Summer 1950

MADE AND PRINTED IN GREAT BRITAIN BY
UNWIN BROTHERS, LTD., THE GRESHAM PRESS
WOKING, SURREY
FOR THE PUBLISHERS, B. T. BATSFORD, LTD.
LONDON: 15 NORTH AUDLEY STREET, W.1, AND MALVERN WELLS, WORCESTER-
SHIRE. NEW YORK: 122 EAST 55TH STREET. TORONTO: 103 ST. CLAIR AVENUE
WEST. SYDNEY: 156 CASTLEREAGH STREET

A NOTE ON THE METHODS AND INFLUENCE OF

C. H. B. AND MARJORIE QUENNELL

ON HISTORY TEACHING IN SCHOOLS

By FRANK ROSCOE, M.A.

Late Secretary of the Royal Society of Teachers

THE subject of history has formed part of the school curriculum for several generations, but it is only during recent years that any serious attempt has been made to enliven it with material likely to interest the young. A century ago schools began the practice of treating the dates of events as all-important while giving little attention to the events themselves.

Readers of Jane Austen will recall the comments made by Maria and Julia Bertram on the attainments of their ten-year-old cousin, Fanny Price:

"How long ago it is since we used to repeat the chronological order of the Kings of England, with the dates of their accession, and most of the principal events of their reigns!"

"Yes," added the other, "and of the Roman Emperors as low as Severus."

At Rugby Arnold introduced a fuller treatment of ancient history, but for long after his death the public schools made little or no attempt to teach English history to their pupils. For younger children Mrs. Markham produced *Little Arthur's History of England* and Charles Dickens wrote *A Child's History of England*. In the later middle of last century there were textbooks more ambitious in scope but even less attractive in form and content. They treated history mainly as a record of dynasties, wars and conquests, ignoring the lives and doings of ordinary men and women.

John Richard Green saw the defects of this kind of treatment, and wrote his *Short History of the English People* as a corrective and an example. His work was extremely useful, but the beneficial influence was limited in the main to students of mature years.

v

The panorama of agrarian and industrial development, changes in social structure, and the gradual growth of national institutions are less dramatic and picturesque than tales of royal persons, glittering pageants and knightly prowess.

The ever-widening scope of historical research has opened many different fields of study. We have to-day many "histories"—ancient, modern, political, social, local, economic, religious or literary, with countless specialised branches such as the history of architecture, of shipping, of games, localities or buildings.

Amid this vast and ill-ordered mass of facts, all falling under the general title "history," some guidance must be given to the young student. Lacking a coherent thread or clue he may be engulfed in confusion, unable to see the wood for the trees. The traditional scheme is the one of which Fanny Price knew nothing. Dates of kings and queens, the principal events of their reigns, and copious attention to "battle, murder and sudden death"—these formed the material of much school history down to a generation ago. Imperfectly retained and distorted in outline, it furnished a sorry equipment of historical knowledge for the British citizen. There was need for a fresh presentation of history which a child could follow with an understanding proper to his years and with that interest which is always aroused when familiar things are seen from a new angle.

The most vivid and striking contribution to the new method of treating history for young students was devised by C. H. B. Quennell, in happy collaboration with his wife, Marjorie Quennell. Neither of them had been through the conventional discipline of historical study and research. She is an artist by training and inclination, while he was an architect to whom the first War brought an interruption of a successful professional career. He had written an excellent handbook on Norwich Cathedral, but he never posed as a literary expert.

His chief interest was in architecture, and in the course of his practice he developed an abiding zest for examples of good workmanship, and a profound respect for skilled craftsmen in every field. The individuality and fitness of the work which they did in the days before mass-production gave him constant pleasure. His desire to convey something of his own knowledge and enthusiasm was the mainspring of his efforts in authorship. Beginning with the charming volumes entitled *A History of Everyday Things in England* (Batsford), he and Mrs. Quennell went on to describe everyday things at different periods and in different places.

It is hardly too much to say that they made history while writing it. By laborious research and careful selection they were able to present the story of people "in their habit as they lived." Skilful illustrations supplemented the text, making the successive volumes doubly interesting. The effect was strengthened by the fortunate choice of a publisher whose skill in the production of books goes far beyond the practice of the maker of cheap "best-sellers." This happy conjunction of author, artist and publisher furnished a memorable and permanent contribution to the list of books available for young students of history. The general run of school text-books might be described as drab in appearance and in contents, but the Quennell books are attractive and even exhilarating in both respects. We need not wonder that they are finding imitators and helping to raise the standard of book-production for schools.

It is fitting that readers of the Quennell books should have in mind a word-picture of the author. Yet it is impossible to convey any adequate impression of the man. His chief characteristic was an unquenchable enthusiasm for things that are "beautiful and of good report." He would journey for miles to see a well-built farm wagon or any good example of handicraft. He had about him no trace of self-assurance nor any of the windy rhetoric used by self-styled connoisseurs on art or architecture. Sometimes he would say, with a rueful smile, that he was too ignorant to understand the meaning of modern developments, but in truth he understood them well enough and formed shrewd estimates of their worth. This will be evident to readers of his last book, *The Good New Days* (Batsford), where he describes modern industrial and agricultural processes and is mindful of their significance as factors in the life of coming generations.

In the memory of those who knew him, C. H. B. Quennell

has an assured place. They will always be able to recall vivid pictures of one who radiated good will towards his fellows, treating their failings with whimsical humour and extracting merriment from circumstances untoward enough to have discouraged a spirit less well armed against fate. He had a blithe heart and an unfailing zest for simple human joys. Children loved him, the sure perception of youth enabling them to see in him one who was ready to share their interests without assuming the airs of a mentor.

This firm link with childhood was of a piece with the man, for he retained to the end the enquiring spirit and quick enthusiasms of youth. He died on December 5, 1935. A fitting epitaph for him might be found in the words of Robert Louis Stevenson:

"Every heart that has beat strong and cheerfully has left a hopeful impulse behind it in the world, and bettered the condition of mankind."

NOTE TO THIRD EDITION (FIFTH IMPRESSION)

The death of my husband at the close of 1935 after twenty years continuous collaboration has meant that I have had to undertake single-handed the revision of this volume for its third edition and fifth impression. As it had to be re-set, I have taken the opportunity to carry out a fairly thorough revision on the lines which I feel he would himself have adopted, eliminating passages and illustrations which could be replaced by matter of greater practical interest, and thus tending to a more systematic treatment, while adding, in collaboration with the Publishers, further colour drawings and half-tone and line illustrations which seemed appropriate and not unattractive, though preserving the main lines of the work unchanged. I can only hope that in its new form the volume will commend itself as in the past to the different circles by whom the series has been appreciated.

LONDON, *September* 1937. M. Q.

NOTE TO FOURTH EDITION (NINTH IMPRESSION)

In the printing of this edition advantage has been taken of the opportunity to correct some slight misprints and to insert one or two additional illustrations.

Spring 1950. THE PUBLISHERS.

FIG. I.—The Tomb of Henry VII

PREFACE

WE should like to start Volume II of our book by thanking our reviewers and readers for their kindly reception of Volume I; the more, because they did not regard it as a picture-book.

Our work has been done for boys and girls of any age, and we hope it will be useful in providing a background for school history lessons, and make the historical figures more real by housing and clothing them, showing the games they played and the things they fashioned. But from our own standpoint we shall have failed, unless we can as well interest our readers in the way things were made, and encourage them to make and do things themselves.

But leaving craftsmanship till later on, we think a great mistake is made in not seeking to interest boys and girls in architecture, costume, and the arts generally. One can so well argue back from the details of church, house, and dress, to the characteristics of the people who have produced them. In Volume I we acknowledged our indebtedness to a chart prepared by Mr. H. F. T. Cooper. This is an exceedingly interesting production. A large sheet of paper has been divided into twenty spaces across its width, by five in its height. This gives 100 spaces, to each of which is allotted ten years. The chart starts at the top left-hand corner and reads across the page, and each column has the names of kings and queens, and of all the splendid work and workmen, for 1000 years. Different coloured inks are used. Architecture is black, and we can trace at the beginning the early work at Winchester, Ely, Tewkesbury, and St. Albans. In the thirteenth century the columns are deep with names of all the cathedrals, but not so much space is occupied in the fourteenth and fifteenth centuries, and Gothic architecture declines with the Church which produced it. Painting is red, and the first entry is Cimabue, b. 1240, then Giotto, b. 1266, and then across the columns and the centuries is a stately procession of those who have sought to express the ideal of beauty. Poets have green; the historians, dramatists, and essayists, purple; but surely the poets should have had the purple patches.

The use of the chart, and we think every school should have, or, better still, make one, is that in a very short time, as one studies the waves of coloured names, there comes a recognition of great movements, which express all the hopes and aspirations of a people. The sturdiness of Norman architecture is as typical as the grace and beauty of the thirteenth-century work. The fourteenth and fifteenth centuries showed little organic structural development, and seemed to have few impulses. Decoration was overlaid on older forms. In this Volume II of our book we have tried to show how all the old building, with its furniture, the dresses of the people, and their games, were not playthings, or the sport of fashion as now, but history in stone, wood, and fabrics.

Then we hope our book may help boys and girls to come to a proper decision as to what "job of work" they will take up later on. The grown-ups have an alarming way of closing down on you, and suddenly demanding, "Now then, what are you going to be?" and one does not know; so far too frequently the naturalist becomes a bank clerk, the tinker a tailor, and the soldier a sailor—which is all so much waste, and the cause of great unhappiness.

We have tried to present work as a joyous sort of business, and here we think our readers may say, "Now we have lost faith in you; it is dull, and dreary—see how miserable the grown-ups look. We convict you of a thumping fabrication." Our reply to this is, that we are quite sure that in the old days the craftsman enjoyed his job, or he would not have taken so much trouble to make quite ordinary things beautiful. If for the last hundred years the reverse has come to be the case, from the historical point of view such a period is only a spasm in the old world's pain; the future belongs to the boys and girls of to-day, and they must alter things, improve them, and think of other things than money.

We should also like to have drawn a parallel between football and architecture, and shown how the best results are obtained by team-work, rather than by the individual star performer. We want to interest our readers in everyday things, because never was there a period in the world's history when these were of greater importance. We are constantly coming up against such phrases nowadays as "Increasing Production" and "Rate of Exchange."

We all know that the Great War meant the sacrifice of many of the best and noblest lives in the country; that we are all richer by this in one way, and much poorer in another needs little emphasis. We have also wasted enormous quantities of the materials we need for living. Our iron, coal, wood, and all kinds of other things, have been wrought into shells, and exploded; built into ships, and sent to the bottom of the sea by enemy submarines. So when the statesmen talk of the necessity for increasing production, they mean of all the materials, and everyday things, we need for our life and trade; not that we need more Treasury notes, or money.

If the thing is more important than money, then it is obvious that while we are increasing production, it will be as well to maintain our reputation for making good things. We can only do this if the makers are happy and contented, and think they are fairly treated.

Now as to what is meant by the "Rate of Exchange." Boys and girls often hear that foreign countries will allow us sometimes more, and sometimes less, for the British pound, and there is some excuse for thinking that it is a rate of exchange of money; but this is not the case—in reality it is our old friend, the everyday thing, that is being exchanged. Let us see how this works. Great Britain is a small place, with a large population, and we cannot produce all our food, or the raw materials we need for our industry; but we possess coal, iron, and clever workmen. We go to South America, and in effect say to the people there, "We will exchange ploughs and locomotives for your corn and cattle"; and this they are glad to do, because they cannot make machinery, and they grow more foodstuffs than they can consume. During the war we could not produce the things which other countries wanted, and offered them money instead, but this was of little use, unless with it, from some other country, they could obtain the desired everyday thing. As these became scarcer all over the world, money had less purchasing power.

The statesmen, then, want to increase production, so that not only may we be able to supply our own needs, but have something over to exchange for raw materials and food. So the everyday thing is more important than money, and triumphs over it, and, such being the case, quite deserves a little history of its own. But our space is limited, our subject large, and our own knowledge small, so we cannot do more than present an outline sketch, and if we can but stimulate our readers' interest, they themselves must fill in those wide open spaces which we have only skirted.

MARJORIE AND C. H. B. QUENNELL

BERKHAMSTED, HERTS
September 1919

Our thanks are due to the friends who have helped us: Mr. H. W. Burrows and Mr. Gentry of Braintree, for information on mills. Mr. A. Rosling of Chelmsford, for the loan of gun-locks from his collection, from which our drawings were made. Mr. R. Morton Nance has again been of the greatest assistance with our ships; and Miss Churchill helped with information as to libraries.

We have gained very much from the following books, and recommend them to such of our readers as desire fuller information on any of the subjects:

A LIST OF USEFUL BOOKS OF REFERENCE

Architecture—
The Styles of English Architecture. Two series of large diagrams and
handbooks. ARTHUR STRATTON (Batsford. 1950.)
The Parish Churches of England. COX and FORD. 1950.
The English Abbey. F. H. CROSSLEY. 1949.
Outline of English Architecture. A. H. GARDNER. 1947.
The Old Churches of London. GERALD COBB and Sir GEOFFREY
WEBB. 1948.
British Architects and Craftsmen, 1600–1830. S. SITWELL. 1948.
Stuart and Georgian Churches, 1603–1837. M. WHIFFEN. 1948.

Agriculture and Gardens—
The Formal Garden in England. REGINALD BLOMFIELD and
F. INIGO THOMAS. (Macmillan, 1892.)
Garden Craft in Europe. H. INIGO TRIGGS. (Batsford, 1910.)
The English Garden. R. DUTTON. 1950.
Oriental Gardening. Sir WILLIAM CHAMBERS. 1772.
Systema Agriculturæ. WORLIDGE. 1669.
England's Improvement. CAPTAIN WALTER BLITH.
Sylva. JOHN EVELYN. (The diarist.)
Horse-Hoeing Husbandry. JETHRO TULL. 1733.
The Implements of Agriculture. J. ALLAN RANSOME. 1843.

Church History—
History of the Cathedral Church of Wells. E. A. FREEMAN. 1870.

Coaches—
History of Coaches. G. A. THRUPP. (Kerby & Endears, 1877.)

Decoration and Furniture—
History of English Furniture. MACQUOID. (Lawrence & Bullen.)
The English Interior. R. DUTTON. 1949.

Dress—
Dress and Habits. JOSEPH STRUTT. 1799.
Historic Costume. FRANCIS M. KELLY and Professor RANDOLPH
SCHWABE. (Batsford, 1925.)
A Short History of Costume and Armour, chiefly in England,
1066–1800. Same authors. 2 vols. (Batsford, 1931.)
English Costume, 1066–1820. D. CLAYTON CALTHROP. 1946.

Houses—
Homes of Other Days. THOMAS WRIGHT. (Trübner & Co.)
Early Renaissance Architecture in England, 1901—Growth of the
English House—The English Home. J. A. GOTCH. (Batsford.)
Later Renaissance Architecture in England. BELCHER and
MACARTNEY. (Batsford.)
The English Country House. R. DUTTON. 1950.
"Country Life," for its splendid illustrations of old work.

Ironwork—
J. STARKIE GARDNER. (Batsford, 1911.)
      „   (H.M. Stationery Office, 1914.)

Libraries—
The Care of Books. J. W. CLARK. (Cambridge Univ. Press.)

Music and Musical Instruments—
A History of Musical Instruments. A. J. HIPKINS and WILLIAM
GIBB. (Adam & Charles Black, 1888.)

Old English Instruments of Music. F. W. GALPIN. (Methuen.)
Plaine and Easy Introduction to Practicale Musicke, set downe in
the form of a Dialogue. 1597.

Schools—
The Schools of Mediæval England. A. F. LEACH. (Methuen, 1915.)
The Old Grammar Schools. FOSTER WATSON. 1916.
The Old Public Schools of England. J. RODGERS. 1938.

Social Life—
English Home Life. CHRISTINA HOLE. 1947.
English Children in the Olden Times. ELIZABETH GODFREY.
Amusements of Old London. W. B. BOULTON.
TRAILL's Social England. (Cassell.)
The Microcosm of London. R. ACKERMANN. 1811.
Microcosm; or, a Picturesque Delineation of the Arts, Agriculture,
Manufactures, etc., of Great Britain. W. H. PYNE. 1803–6.
Londina Illustrata. ROBERT WILKINSON. 1819.
DOUCE's Illustrated Shakespeare.
Progresses and Pageants of Queen Elizabeth.
Through England on a Side Saddle. (The Diary of CELIA FIENNES.)
By the Hon. Mrs. GRIFFITHS. 1888. New Edition edited by
C. Morris. 1947.
Old English Household Life. G. JEKYLL and S. R. JONES. 1948.
England in Tudor Times. L. F. SALZMAN. (Batsford.)
The Life and Work of the English People, 12–18th Centuries.
DOROTHY HARTLEY and M. ELLIOT. 6 vols. (Batsford.)

Sports—
English Sports and Pastimes. CHRISTINA HOLE. 1949.
Sports and Pastimes. JOSEPH STRUTT. 1810.
Old English Sporting Prints and Books.
The Booke of Hunting. TURBERVILLE. 1576. (Oxford, 1908.)
The Booke of Falconrie. TURBERVILLE. 1575.
Gentleman's Recreation. R. BLOME. 1686.

Toys—
Toys of Other Days. Mrs. NEVILLE JACKSON.
Children's Toys of Bygone Days. By KARL GRÖBER. (Batsford.)

NOTE OF ACKNOWLEDGMENT TO THIRD EDITION

MY thanks are due to the British Museum for the drawing on Plate 25,
and the Victoria and Albert Museum for the paintings reproduced on
Plates 33, 38, 39 (2). I am indebted to Mr. Sydney R. Jones for Fig. 16,
from his "English Village Homes," in the Batsford "British Heritage"
series. Plates 9 and 22 were taken for the publishers by the late Will F.
Taylor, and Plates 31 and 32 from Blome's "Gentleman's Recreation"
were reproduced from a copy kindly provided by Messrs. J. and E.
Bumpus Ltd. Plate 33 (top) is by Messrs. Bedford Lemere & Co. Most
of the other engravings are from material in the publishers' collection.

M. Q.

CONTENTS

CHAPTER I.—"Tudor" Period of Design, 1500–1599.

Sixteenth Century.

Dates.	Kings and Queens of England and France.	Famous Men.	Great Events.	Principal Buildings.
1500	Henry VII. and *Louis XII.*	Hans Holbein *b.* 1497.—P.	. . . . .	Layer Marney Towers, Essex, 1500–25
1501	. . . .	Benvenuto Cellini *b.*—S.	Marriage of Arthur and Katherine of Arragon	East Barsham, Norfolk, 1501–15
1502	. . . .		Marriage of Margaret and James IV. of Scotland	
1503	. . . .	Sir Thomas Wyatt *b.*		
1504	. . . .	Grocyn—W.		
1506	. . . .	Colet, Dean of St. Paul's		
1508	. . . .			King's College, Cambridge
1509	Henry VIII., *m.* Katherine of Arragon; Anne Boleyn; Jane Seymour; Anne of Cleves; Katherine Howard; Katherine Parr			St. Paul's School founded
1510	. . . .	Erasmus—W.		
1511	. . . .	Sir Thomas More—W.	More writes *Utopia*	Westminster Abbey, Henry VII.'s
1513	. . . .	Cardinal Wolsey	Battle of Spurs, and Battle of Flodden	Chapel
1514	. . . .		Wolsey made Archbishop	Hampton Court, 1514–40
1515	*Francis I.*	Roger Ascham *b.*—W.		
1516	. . . .		Publication of Erasmus' translation of the Testament, and More's *Utopia*	Henry VII.'s tomb
1518	. . . .	Palladio *b.*—A.		House . . .
1519	. . . .	Martin Luther	Luther's Objections	Compton Wynyates
1520	. . . .		Field of Cloth of Gold	
1521	. . . .		"Diet" at Worms	
1522	. . . .		Luther publishes translation of Testament	
1523	. . . .			Sutton Place, Guildford, 1523–25
1525	. . . .			Hengrave Hall, Suffolk, 1526–38
1526	. . . .	John Calvin		
1529	. . . .		Fall of Wolsey	Ford's Hospital, Coventry
1530	. . . .		Death of Wolsey	
1533	. . . .		Divorce of Katherine	
1535	. . . .		Death of More. Death of Erasmus. Execution of Anne Boleyn	
1536	. . . .	Robert Aske	Suppression of smaller Monasteries, 1536–40. Pilgrimage of Grace	
1539	. . . .		Suppression of great Monasteries	
1540	. . . .	Stephen Gardiner	Fall of Cromwell	Lacock Abbey, Wilts
1541	. . . .			Berkhamsted School founded
1542	. . . .	John Knox	War with Scotland. Battle of Solway Moss	
1543	. . . .		War with France	
1544	. . . .	Cranmer		
1545	. . . .		Confiscation of the Chantries	
1547	Edward VI. and *Henry II.*		Execution of Surrey	
1549	. . . .	Hugh Latimer		
1550	. . . .	Isaac Oliver	Peace with France and Scotland	Sherborne School founded
1551	. . . .			Shrewsbury School founded
1552	. . . .	Sir W. Raleigh *b.*		Bedford School founded
		Edmund Spenser *b.*—Pt.		
1553	Mary		Lady Jane Grey proclaimed Queen	
1554	. . . .	Sir Philip Sidney *b.*—Pt.	Wyatt's Rebellion. Execution of Lady Jane Grey	
1555	. . . .	Cardinal Pole		
1556	. . . .	Ridley		
1557	. . . .			Repton School founded
1558	Elizabeth		Loss of Calais	Moreton Old Hall, Cheshire
1559	*Francis II.*			
1560	*Charles IX.*			
1561	Regency *of Catherine de Medici*	Francis Bacon *b.*—W.	Mary Stuart returns to Scotland	
1564	. . . .	William Shakespeare *b.*		
1565	. . . .	Christopher Marlowe *b.*—Pt.	Mary Stuart marries Darnley	Highgate School founded
1567	. . . .		Murder of Darnley. Mary marries Bothwell	Longleat, Wilts
1568	. . . .		Mary imprisoned. Escapes to England	Rugby School founded
1569	. . . .		Rising in the North	
1570	. . . .		Pope excommunicates Elizabeth	Middle Temple Hall
1571	. . . .			Harrow School founded
1572	. . . .	Inigo Jones *b.*—A.		Burghley House, Northants
1573	. . . .	Ben Jonson *b.*—W.		
1574	*Henry III.*			
1576	. . . .			Hardwick Hall
1577	. . . .	Peter Paul Rubens *b.*—P.	Drake sails round the world	
1580	. . . .	Franz Hals *b.*—P.		Montacute
1583	. . . .			Barlboro' House, Derbyshire
1584	. . . .			Uppingham School founded
1585	. . . .			Doddington Hall, Lincolnshire
1586	. . . .		English expedition to the Netherlands	
1587	. . . .	Hawkins	Babington's Plot. Execution of Mary, Queen of Scots	
1588	. . . .	Drake	Arrival and defeat of the Spanish Armada	
1589	*Henry IV.*	Sir Humphrey Gilbert	Publication of *Faerie Queene*	
1590	. . . .	Sir Martin Frobisher		
1591	. . . .	Robert Herrick *b.*—Pt.		
1593	. . . .	Izaak Walton *b.*—W.		Trinity College, Cambridge, Neville's Court
1596	. . . .		Attack on Cadiz	
1598	. . . .	Velasquez *b.* 1599.—P.	Rebellion of Tyrone	Condover House, Shropshire
1599	. . . .	Sir A. Van Dyck *b.*—P.	Essex goes to Ireland	Broughton Castle, Oxon

A.=Architect. P.=Painter. Pt.=Poet. S.=Sculptor. W.=Writer.

17th-Century Chart, p. 80. 18th Century Chart, p. 148.

PLATE 2

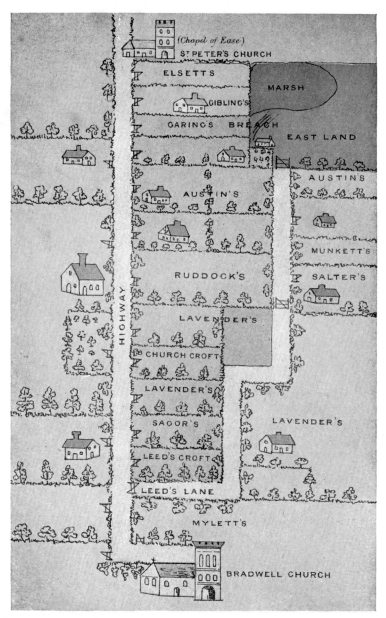

From a Contemporary Survey

Elizabethan Crofts at Bradwell-on-Sea, Essex

PLATE 3

Engraving by J. Nel, 1589

Orchestral Concert, with virginal, viol, viola-da-gamba, recorders, flute, trombones and lute

Engraving by Weidetz, 1535

A Horde of Beggars invading a Town

FIG. 2.—Horseman at the Field of the Cloth of Gold
Horseman, Restoration, Fig. 47; Horseman, Georgian, Fig. 80

CHAPTER I

THE SIXTEENTH CENTURY

THE sixteenth century is of the greatest interest to us, because it marks the change from the Middle Ages to the modern world we now live in, and this change, though not heralded by conquest, was in reality a far greater one than that which followed the coming of the Normans in 1066. In Vol. I we said that the Conqueror was responsible for the introduction into England of a new set of ideas, and in the same way the sixteenth century marked a general change of

I   B spirit, which altered the whole outlook of the people and therefore the appearance of everyday things.

William's new ideas of 1066 were carefully grafted on to those of the Anglo-Saxons. He knit the country together by Feudalism. This, at its best, was something very good, because it was the acceptance of the principle of service. The faith of men was not disturbed, but rather strengthened, by the work of good men like Lanfranc and Anselm. Froude, the nineteenth-century historian, said the Churchmen ruled the State, and "they were allowed to rule because they deserved to rule, and in the fullness of reverence kings and nobles bent before a power which was nearer to God than their own." Things were done and made, land was held, and lives lived more in common than nowadays; to borrow was thriftless, to lend usury. The Gothic cathedral was the work, not of one man, but of many, and still remains as one of the finest conceptions of mankind.

Towards the end of the Middle Ages people had become restless, the old standards were being overthrown, and there did not seem any fit to take their place. In the old days men had worked together, and accepted the principle of service; for the latter the sixteenth century substituted that of competition. It was thought that if man worked against man, then everybody's wits would be sharpened, and the world go forward. The individual begins to step out of the crowd and beckon to us.

Froude contrasts the difference between the two ideals in this way: "In these times of ours, well-regulated selfishness is the recognized rule of action—every one of us is expected to look out first for himself, and take care of his own interests. At the time I speak of, the Church ruled the State with the authority of a conscience, and self-interest, as a motive of action, was only named to be abhorred"—but this was written in 1867, and would not be so true now as it was then. If it were possible for a boy or girl, who reads this book, to meet a boy who went to the sixteenth-century school, illustrated in Fig. 13, they would find they had a great deal in common, not only in the things they used, but what is more important, in the things they thought about. But if our readers could be

2

taken back to the Eton that Henry VI founded, then the case would be reversed, and one boy would not understand the other at all; their outlook on life would be quite different.

It may help us to understand better the position of affairs at the beginning of the sixteenth century if we consider how social life was divided up.

William Harrison in 1577 placed the people of England into four classes, namely: gentlemen, that is, princes, lords, men of title, and squires or country gentlemen holding land; citizens or burgesses, these comprising the new class that was rapidly rising and becoming of increasing importance, the merchants and traders, the vast new middle class of England, trading at home and overseas, and peopling the City of London.

Then came the farmers and yeomen, cultivators and producers of the goods sold and of foodstuffs; and lastly the artificers and labourers who worked for hire but did not own. These men, formerly villeins, by the end of the reign of Henry VIII were nearly all free men. Land was changing hands; the suppression of the monasteries and the transference of large tracts of land to the Crown, and from there by gift or purchase to new owners, led to diminution of cultivation.

These men, to whom the land was a commercial asset and not a personal inheritance, led by the increasing importance of the wool trade, grazed sheep instead of cultivating, even enclosing common land, thereby halving the labour needed and throwing many out of work. For this reason also, rents began to be paid in money instead of work, later the cause of much difficulty, for whereas a man could pay his landlord by working certain hours for him, it was vastly more difficult to find outside work with pay in order to find the money for the rent. Elizabeth, to help the cause of the labourers, passed a law that no cottage was to be built in less than four acres of land, trying in this way to give them some means of livelihood. Many a poor man planted on this land cabbages, radishes, turnips, parsnips, carrots, melons, pompons (pumpkins), and kept a pig or cow; "by which," as William Harrison says, "he and his poor household liveth as their principal food, sith, they can do no better." A collection of

3

Elizabethan small holdings is seen in Pl. 2, which is taken from a contemporary map of part of the parish of Bradwell-on-Sea, Essex.

Harrison speaks of the growing evils connected with increasing trade. He says that whereas in past times men made goods and sold them, now middlemen in the markets eat up the grower's profits, that purveyors take up butter, eggs, cheese, pigs, capons, hens, chickens, hogs, bacon, and such-like in one market, and suffer their wives to sell them in another or to the poulterers of London.

"Whereby," he says, "also I gather that the maintenance of a superfluous number of dealers in most trades is one of the greatest causes why the prices of things become excessive."

Markets were held once a week in all towns and all things needed for household use were to be sold and bought there; large fairs were usually held once or twice in the year.

Shops were increasing rapidly in the towns, and these were usually a single room level with the street, the shutter of which let down to form a counter and a sign hung above denoted the trade. At first the room behind was often used for the making of the goods to be sold, but as time went on the shop became the place where goods were "brought" to be sold, rather than "made" to be sold.

As the towns grew, new houses were erected with little regard to space or place, and the streets became narrow and overcrowded. Generally ill paved, with all the house rubbish thrown out into them, and ill lit except where the wealthier inhabitants were obliged by law to hang out lanthorns, the streets cannot have been pleasant to walk in. During the latter half of the sixteenth century, scavengers and dust-carts were appointed to clear the rubbish in the streets, and a number of leading citizens were bound to keep leather buckets of water and great fish hooks in readiness in case of fire. Two force pumps worked with wheels were also set up to supply the city with water, also a help in case of fire, which was a great danger in the narrow congested streets of wooden or timber-framed houses.

With distress in the country the labourers moved towards the town, and overcrowding grew and with it slums. Parts of London became plague spots of poverty; filth and vice were rampant. A law was made "One house one family," but it was a law impossible to enforce in the rabbit warrens of housing, and another legislation forbade the erection of buildings on hitherto unoccupied parts of the city. But these measures were powerless to stem the influx of the unemployed and unemployable, or to prevent their herding together in the dark and obscure parts of the town. Citizens out after dark dared not venture unaccompanied, and with lanterns and swords prepared themselves for any chance encounter with robbers or cut-throats lurking in the shadows on their way home. Many of these unemployed joined together into great bands and roamed over the countryside, pilfering, robbing, and terrifying whole villages with their lawless numbers.

Fig. 3.—Vagabonds, 1609
(v. also Pl. 3)

The nursery rhyme "The beggars are coming to London Town" (Pl. 3) was then no mere jingle, but a menace which caused all the citizens on the outskirts to put up their shutters and to barricade themselves in their houses, driving so far as was possible their beasts into safety. Edward VI was so moved by a sermon of Bishop Ridley concerning the plight of the great poverty-stricken hordes in parts of London, that he wrote to the Lord Mayor and through him a committee was formed to inquire into the matter and finally three houses were founded, "Graie Friars," now Christ's Hospital for poor children, St. Thomas of Southwark, and St. Bartholomew in Smithfield for at least 200 diseased persons; and Bridewell, a prison to punish idle and vagabond persons. In 1569 there was such a horde of beggars approaching London that the corporation being apprised of it, beadles were appointed to watch for them to send off the able-bodied to Bridewell, the diseased to St. Bartholomew's Hospital, and the children to Christ's Hospital.

Henry VII had served an apprenticeship of poverty and knew the value of money; he was not to be tempted into wars abroad, unless he could make them pay, but preferred to devote all his attention to home affairs.

Certainly when he died in 1509, he left England in an infinitely better position than when he came to the throne, and he had safely bridged the transitional period between the Middle Ages and the Renaissance.

Bacon said of the first Tudor king, that he deserved to rank with Louis XI of France and Ferdinand of Aragon as "the three magi of kings of these ages."

Now let us pass to a consideration of the everyday things in England in the sixteenth century, and see what the people looked like.

The coloured plate, Pl. 4, shows the costume of the time. In Vol. I we saw how the middle part of the fifteenth century was a period of great extravagance, and dress was made to distort rather than clothe the figure. Men's garments either trailed on the ground or were cut excessively short, headdresses were monstrous, and shoes so long and pointed that they were fastened up to the knee. It is curious to notice how each period has its own type of design, and how this runs through everything made during that time. The detail of

FIG. 4.—Fforstaller and Regrator of Marketts and Feyres and Vitellars,* 1509

* Fforstaller was one who bought goods on the way to market; Regrator one who created a corner in goods in the market. A certain cure for profiteering.

6

PLATE 4

Costume.   Sixteenth Century

Seventeenth-Century Costume, Pl. 16.   Eighteenth-Century Costume, Pl. 35, 36, and 37

fifteenth-century architecture was reflected in the dress, and
when the Renaissance came, the somewhat pointed forms of
the Gothic period changed and became like the architecture,
round and fuller in character.

Now in the reign of Edward IV this spirit of extravagance
began to die out, and dress therefore became gradually simpler.
This continued until the end of the reign of Henry VII, to
which period belong the first two figures of our illustration,
Pl. 4. Notice the dress of the lady. The surcoat has quite
disappeared, and her gown is simple. The bodice is cut square
to show the white partelet at the neck, and fits the figure
closely. The sleeves are full and the skirt is gathered into the
waist with a jewelled belt. Under-sleeves were worn, probably
attached separately. The high head-dress has given place to a
flat kerchief-like covering. The man standing with this lady
wears a flat velvet cap and a tunic and hose covered by a
loose full gown with hanging sleeves. Notice his shoes, which
are simpler and more natural in shape than hitherto. In these
two figures we have a good example of a style in its inter-
mediate stage, before it has had time to become exaggerated,
and so spoilt.

The second lady belongs to the next reign, that of Henry
VIII. Her bodice is stiffened, also the skirt, which is open in
the front to show a richly embroidered kirtle. Her hanging
sleeves are fastened back so that the beautiful brocaded lining
is displayed. The under-sleeves are slit from elbow to wrist
and puffed with lawn. For the first time we see ruffles at the
wrist. The kerchief has been altered and the ends are caught
up on to the top, forming a three-cornered head-dress.

The interchange of courtesies between Henry VIII and the
French Court led to a great influx of French fashions, and
men's dress became extremely rich and heavy. Every garment
worn by the second man in this illustration is wonderfully
slashed, laced, and embroidered. The outer coat is of velvet
or heavy silk, and is lined with fur; the short breeches or
trunks hidden by his doublet are of the same material. The
sleeves are bolstered and slashed. The doublet or inner coat
is also richly trimmed, and though in this illustration it is
closed, it was often opened to display a richly embroidered

shirt or French chemay beneath. The slashed shoes are very broad. The flat velvet cap is plumed, and the gentleman's hair is closely cut, following the French fashion rigorously enforced at the court of Henry VIII.

The third couple belong to the reign of Queen Elizabeth. Dresses were slowly becoming stiffer, more ungainly, and more covered with ornament, until the climax came in the shape of the monstrous wheeled farthingale, which came into being towards the latter half of Elizabeth's reign, and lasted well on into the reign of James I. This farthingale consisted of a very full gathered skirt which was stretched out over a large hoop round the hips, falling from that, straight to the ground—a very ungainly and ugly fashion. Bodices were stiff and peaked, and amongst wealthy women embroidered with gold and jewels to an extraordinary degree (see Pl. 4). Ruffs are of Spanish origin. They began as cambric collars (notice the second man's costume), and became larger and more pleated and wired, until similar to those on the third couple in the picture; these, however, are very moderate, both in shape and size. Special sticks were used to plait these ruffs, called pokesticks. An alternative fashion to this was the wearing of large, fan-like collars, made in lawn or cambric, these materials being first brought to England in this reign. These fan-shaped collars reached immense proportions, sometimes two or three layers of cambric being used, each wired to stand stiffly up and away from the head. An example is shown on the ladies in the hall (Fig. 28).

An interesting little account of Queen Elizabeth's clothing as a child, is given in a letter from Lady Bryan, found amongst State papers of the period. After Anne Boleyn's disgrace and death, the Princess Elizabeth was put under the care of Lady Bryan, and was apparently rather neglected by her father, Henry VIII, and those at Court, for Lady Bryan writes asking for clothing for the little girl. She says: "She (Elizabeth) hath neither gown, nor kirtle, nor peticoat, nor no manner of linen, nor fore-smocks (pinafores), nor kerchiefs, nor rails (night-dress), nor body stitchets (corsets), nor handkerchiefs, nor sleeves, nor mufflers, nor biggens (caps)." We must remember that children wore just the same clothing as their elders, so that the inventory of a child's needs would be nearly identical with that of a grown-up person. Many tales could be told of Elizabeth's gowns when she was a Queen, and if she lacked clothes in her youth she certainly made up for it in later years, and on her death, an inventory showed 1000 dresses in her wardrobe.

An account of the dress that Mary Queen of Scots wore to her execution, may be found interesting, perhaps to girls:

"Then did she apparel herself after this manner, in borrowed hair, having on her head a dressing of lawn edged with bone lace and above that a vail (veil) of the same, bowed out with weir (wire), and her cuffs suitable; and about her neck, a pomander chain and an Agnus Dei hanging at a black ribband, a crucifix in her hand, a pair of beads at her girdle with a golden cross at the end. Her uppermost gown was of black satin, printed, training upon the ground, with long hanging sleeves trimmed with akorn buttons of jet and pearl, the sleeves over her arms being cut, to give sight to a pair of purple velvet underneath; her kirtle, as her gown, was of black printed satin: her bodice of crimson satin unlaced in the back, the skirt being of crimson velvet: her stockings of worsted, watchet, clocked, and edged at the top with silver, and under them a pair of white: her shoes of Spanish leather with the rough side outward."

The gown spoken of here would be a garment often worn at this time, and sometimes called a mandeville. One can still be seen at the Victoria and Albert Museum, South Kensington. It was a long mantle or tunic open and unfastened in the front, with long unused sleeves, the arm coming through an opening by the shoulder.

To return, though, to Pl. 4. The third lady wears a feathered hat, and under it the small French hood brought into fashion by Anne of Cleves, and still worn. The hair was as a rule elaborately curled and dressed high, and was often covered with a jewelled caul or net. Many laws were in force regarding dress, and at this time citizens' wives were obliged to wear white knitted caps of woollen yarn, unless their husbands could prove themselves to be gentlemen by descent. In the reign of Queen Mary, all London apprentices wore blue gowns

9

in winter and blue cloaks in summer, with breeches of white broadcloth and flat caps. Servants might not wear their gowns longer than to the calf of the leg.

The third man in our illustration wears a peaked doublet, of the same shape as that worn by the lady. It is, like that of his companion, elaborately ornamented, and the sleeves are padded. He wears trunks, which are the very short stuffed breeches, trunk hose which reach to above the knee, and hose or stockings. These trunk hose are the beginning of the breeches of later days, and mark the end of the long chausses of mediæval times. A later type of Elizabethan dress will be seen in the illustration of the hall, Fig. 28, where some of the men wear no trunks, but trunk hose and hose, the former padded until they resemble bolsters; see also Fig. 36. Later still, the padding was omitted, but the fullness retained, and they were then called galligaskins, gradually becoming narrower until they developed into the full breeches worn by the Cavaliers. Short cloaks to the hip were largely in use, and were often made of perfumed leather. Notice also that the gentleman's shoes have heels, and more nearly approach to modern ones than any before.

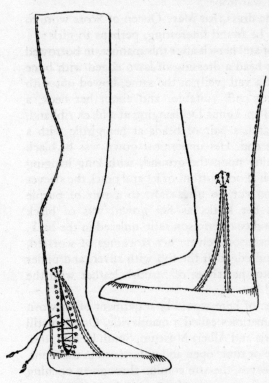

FIG. 5.—A Linen Stocking

Fig. 5 shows a very interesting unbleached linen stocking from a private collection. The material is cut on the cross, which means that the warp threads do not run vertically up and down on the stocking, which is consequently a little more elastic. The stocking is shaped and seamed at the back, and stitched with green silk. The sole is cut larger than the foot, as a separate piece, and brought up and gathered to the shape of the foot, and sewn to the upper portion. Gussets are inserted in each side, the seams having ornamental stitchery of green silk. On the outside, the back seam of the gusset is left open to make the ankle large enough for the passage of the foot, and the gusset then closed by drawing up a green silk cord, through green silk eyelet holes, and tied at the top, which is finished with a clock to prevent the material splitting; and the clock still remains as an ornament on stockings of to-day.

Having gained some idea of the appearance of sixteenth-century men or women, we will now consider their doings. We said in the introduction that even the appearance of every-day things was altered, and this was not to satisfy capricious fancy, but because the life of the time was altered, and the things used reflected this.

In the fifteenth-century chart we noted how the Turks captured Constantinople in 1453; one result of this was that scholars from that city, where the Greek tradition had never wholly died away, fled to other parts of Europe. In Italy they formed a school of learning which became interested in Greek literature. Caxton started printing at Westminster in 1476, and this helped to spread here what was called the Revival of Learning. Grocyn, a Fellow of New College, gave Greek lectures at Oxford. It is very difficult for us to understand now, how wonderful these must have seemed to people knowing only mediæval literature; perhaps boys and girls can judge a little by remembering their first impression of, say, "The Frogs," by Aristophanes. The difference is much like the two sorts of type used for printing. The former is black letter, very decorative to look at but difficult to read; the latter, expressed by Greek and Roman characters, clear and simple.

Erasmus, born in 1467, was first a monk, but obtained release from his vows from Julius II. He came to England in 1497 and met Sir Thomas More and Dean Colet. The influence of these men was to be tremendous, and they were all very learned, sincere, and good. Erasmus said: "I have given up my whole soul to Greek learning, and as soon as I get any money I shall buy Greek books—and then I shall buy some clothes"; and of More he said, "When did Nature mould a

FIG. 6.—An Apprentice going to draw water, 1572

temper more gentle, endearing, and happy than the temper of Thomas More?" We must remember that though these men wished to reform the Church, they had no desire to break away from its teaching; the course the Reformation took in the end was repugnant to them, and Sir Thomas More laid down his life rather than surrender his principles.

Had men been wise enough to accept Sir Thomas More as the champion of the Reformation, we can judge from the pages of *Utopia*,*

which he wrote in 1516, of the kindlier spirit which might have been brought to bear on the problems of the Church. In *Utopia* we read that "it should be lawfull for everie man to favoure and folow what religion he would, and that he mighte do the best he could to bring other to his opinion, so that he did it peaceablie, gentelie, and soberlie, without hastie and contentious rebuking and inveihing against other. If he could not by faire and gentle speche induce them unto his opinion yet he should use no kinde of violence, and refraine from displeasaunte and seditious woordes." Erasmus was rendered miserable by standing between the two extreme parties; like More and Colet, he realised that the Church

* *Utopia* deals with More's conception of the Ideal State.

12

needed reformation, but hated the methods by which it was accomplished.

When we were writing Vol. I it occurred to us that one of the first things of importance which must be described was the ship; because with its aid William gained possession of the Narrow Seas, and was so enabled to defeat Harold at the battle of Hastings. It was an early illustration of what is meant by Sea Power. In Vol. II we must do much the same, and give early consideration to the Navy, because with its aid we maintained in the sixteenth century our hold on the Channel, and defeated the Armada. Had it not done so, then all the things we are going to illustrate would have been cut to a different pattern. However, this is not a real history book, so boys and girls who want to know what "English Seamen of the Sixteenth Century" were like, should read the splendid book by Froude which bears this title.

We can only give an outline. Columbus discovered America in 1492, and Spain benefited by this to an extraordinary extent. Ferdinand had laid solid foundations for her power, and on these an empire was built which stretched across to the New World. The Spaniard ruled the seas, though challenged by us, and continued so to do until in 1588 came the great trial of strength, and the Armada was defeated. We were enabled to do this because we had fine seamen and ships. It will be interesting to see how this came about. All the nations had been stimulated by the discovery of America, and fabulous tales were told of the wealth to be obtained there.

Fig. 7 shows what a hazy idea the old navigators had of the shape of the New World, and the terrors, like cannibalism, which they imagined existed there.

The Revival of Learning led to an intense interest and curiosity in other people's doings; a spirit of adventure was in the air. Wise old Henry VII realised all this, and the necessity for being up and doing. The first English expedition to America sailed in 1497, under John Cabot. Henry built the *Regent*, and the *Sovereign*, both larger and more powerful than any ships which had gone before. The *Great Harry*, launched in 1514, was the wonder of her day, and Henry VIII, assisted by Wolsey, continued the good work of his father, and can

Fig. 7.—The New World

Ptolemy, Geographia Universalis, 1540

probably be regarded as the founder of the Navy. Before this, ships had been provided by the Cinque Ports. He greatly encouraged the seamen of his time, and William Hawkins sailed under his flag to Guinea; later, in Elizabeth's time, his son, Sir John Hawkins, engaged in the slave trade, and opened the route to the West Indies. In 1577 Drake sailed out of Plymouth Sound in the *Pelican*, of only 120 tons, the *Elizabeth*, of eighty tons, and two sloops, of fifty and thirty tons. He sailed clean round the world, and gave the Spaniards some cause for alarm, because they saw that presently a nation which could produce such sailors would challenge them, and that it meant a fight. This was the training which had gone before the Armada, and produced the men and the ships.

In Vol. I we saw how the Crusaders, going into the Eastern seas, were

FIG. 8.—Sailing Diagram

struck by the greater development in shipbuilding they found there, and the northern men adopted the lateen, or leg-of-mutton sail, as part of their rig in the fifteenth century. The reason for their doing so was that it enabled them to sail a little closer to the wind, and made it easier to work their ships. Take the diagram, Fig. 8. The right-hand side of the diagram represents the best that a mediæval boat fitted only with square sails could do. She was at her *best* with the wind right aft. The left-hand side of the diagram illustrates a cutter or hoy rig, which is fore and aft and descended from the lateen. Here one is not hampered by yards and shrouds, and the boat can get to within four points of the wind. But the fore and aft was at its *worst* with the wind due aft; a combination of the two rigs was what the old men aimed at. They did not at once develop the lateen into triangular head-sails, stay-sails, and spanker; this was only done gradually, as we shall see by the illustrations. What they did do in the

FIG. 9.—A Mediterranean Galley

Other illustrations of ships—

Galleon, Fig. 10. *Ark Royal*, Fig. 11. Seventeenth-Century Ship, Fig. 53.
Eighteenth-Century Ship, Fig. 85. Clipper, Fig. 86

fifteenth and sixteenth centuries was to adapt the lateen to the
mizzen and Bonaventure mizzen, and the idea of this must
have been to enable them to change over from one tack to
the other more readily; it could hardly have been to lay their
ships closer to the wind, because the hulls were not high
enough in the bows to make the attempt desirable.

Fig. 9 is of a Mediterranean galley, and has been drawn
from a model at the Science Museum at South Kensington,
which is supposed to have belonged to the Knights of Malta.
Though later in date than the sixteenth century, it can be
taken as typical of the Eastern galley, which influenced the
design of the Elizabethan galleons. Here it should be explained
that galleon meant a man-of-war; gallease was a smaller boat,
like the frigate later on. So far as the galley illustrated is
concerned, it has the beak head, used for ramming, and the

16

PLATE 5

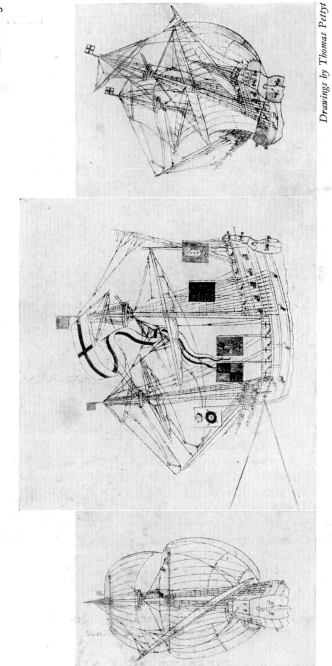

Drawings by Thomas Pettyt

Ships in Calais Harbour

PLATE 6

Seventeenth-Century Barn at Church Farm,
Edlesborough, Buckinghamshire

forecastle. Then the main deck, with twenty-two long sweeps each side for use in calm weather; these were manned by slaves, who sat on benches several to each sweep. Up and down the deck a raised gangway ran between the benches, from whence the overseers could wield their whips against any slave not pulling his weight.

In the tale *Westward Ho!* Salvation Yeo is made to say, when telling his experiences to Sir Richard Grenville and Amyas Leigh: "I must have two hundred stripes in the public place, and then go to the galleys for seven years. And there, gentlemen, ofttimes I thought that it had been better for me to have been burned at once and for all: but you know as well as I, what a floating hell of heat and cold, hunger and thirst, stripes and toil, is every one of those accursed craft."

Now the build of the hull of the galley influenced ship design for a long time, as we shall see, and we have already discussed the influence of the lateen or leg-of-mutton sails which are shown furled on the foremast, mainmast, and mizzen.

The galley's length is given as 165 feet, breadth 22 feet.

The next illustration (Fig. 10) is of an Elizabethan galleon with a beak head closely resembling the galley, forecastle, and high poop. The amusing little turrets, and the ornament, show how closely related the architecture of the sea was to that of the land. The open stern galley is a new feature. So far as rig is concerned, we now have a spritsail on the bowsprit. The foremast and mainmast were square rigged, and the principal interest is in the lateen sails on the mizzen and Bonaventure mizzen. Nettings were used over the waist of the ship as a defence against boarders. Sometimes the ends of the bowsprit, and yards, were provided with hooks to catch in and cut the enemy's rigging when at close quarters. The sails are shown with detachable bonnets laced on, which could be removed instead of reefing. It was at this period that topmasts were arranged so that they could be lowered.

Fig. 11 is of the *Ark Royal*, drawn from a print at the British Museum. This fine boat was built for Sir Walter Raleigh in 1587, but was sold to Queen Elizabeth for £5000. She was the flagship of the fleet which defeated the Armada,

FIG. 10.—An Elizabethan Galleon

Galley, Fig. 9. *Ark Royal*, Fig. 11. Seventeenth-Century Ship, Fig. 53
Eighteenth-Century Ship, Fig. 85.   Clipper, Fig. 86

and as such, entitled to our respectful consideration. Her
tonnage was 800, and crew 400; in 1608 she was rebuilt and
named the *Anne Royal*. Froude gives us a picture of the memorable council of war which was held in the main cabin of the
Ark, on Sunday afternoon, August 8, 1588. The Armada had
been chased up Channel, and if left undisturbed would have
recovered and been ready for Parma and his troops at Dunkirk,
so "Howard, Drake, Seymour, Hawkins, Martin Frobisher,
and two or three others met to consult, knowing that on them
at that moment were depending the liberties of England."
How they decided on fire ships, and the effect of these on the
Spaniards' nerves, is matter for abler pens than we possess;
our main concern is to show something of the appearance of
the *Ark*.

Her hull was still on galley lines, and here it can be noted
how the term quarter-deck came about. There is, starting

18

FIG. 11.—The *Ark Royal*

Galley, Fig. 9.   Galleon, Fig. 10.   Seventeenth-Century Ship, Fig. 53.
Eighteenth-Century Ship, Fig. 85.   Clipper, Fig. 86

from the bows, first the forecastle, then the waist of the ship;
of the remaining part, the first half was called the half-deck,
the next portion the quarter-deck, because it occupied roughly
one-quarter of the space, the remaining portion aft was the
poop. The rig is the same as that described for the galleon,
only the mizzens are more liberally provided with lateen sails.

Pl. 5 is very interesting. The three very jolly little drawings
date from 1545, and were made by Thomas Pettyt; they are
in the Cotton MSS. at the British Museum, and their reference
is Aug. 1, vol. ii. 57B. They are proof that men were beginning
to get life and movement into their drawings.

Elizabeth continued the wise policy of her father and grand-
father, and encouraged trade. She granted the first charter to
the East India Company in 1600, and so laid the foundation
of our Eastern Empire. There were only five ships in the
first fleet of the Company which sailed, and the largest of

these, by name the *Dragon*, was only of 600 tons, with a crew of 202.

Hakluyt, who published a book of voyages, talking of English trade in the sixteenth century, says the ships of London, Southampton, and Bristol traded with Sicily, Tripoli, and Beirut in Syria, carrying these "fine kerseys (cloth)* of divers colours, coarse kerseys, white western dozens, cottons, certain cloths called statutes and others called cardinal whites, and calf-skins, which were well sold in Sicily." They brought back silks, camlets, rhubarb, Malmseys, muscadels, and other wines, sweet oils, cotton, wood, Turkey carpets, galls, pepper, cinnamon, and other spices.

The sixteenth century is also noteworthy for its voyages of discovery. The N.E. and N.W. Passages were thought to lead to India. Sir Hugh Willoughby was one of the first of the discoverers to lay down his life in this cause. Hakluyt tells us that the sixteenth-century sailormen found that, in tropic seas, "a kind of worm is bred which many times pierceth and eateth through the strongest oak that is; therefore that the mariners might be free and safe from this danger, they cover a piece of the keel of the ship with thin sheets of lead."

If the sixteenth century is memorable for its English seamen, it has another claim on our attention, in that so many schools were then founded, or re-established. Starting with St. Paul's, 1509, we have Berkhamsted, 1541, Sherborne, 1550, Shrewsbury, 1551, Bedford, one of the sixteen schools founded by Edward VI, 1552, Repton, 1557, Highgate, 1565, Rugby, 1567, Harrow, 1571, Uppingham, 1584, and many others.

The Tudors, who were themselves very well educated, determined that their subjects should enjoy the same privilege; in many cases the buildings they provided are still serving the same purpose.

There is, however, a general tendency to think that grammar schools did not exist before this time, and that education was in the hands of the monks, but this was not so. We saw in Vol. I how the Benedictine monastery had a training school for novices who wished to become monks, and sometimes another in connection with the almonry, where poor boys

* From Kersey, the cloth village in Suffolk.

were trained for the choir. The precentor taught them singing, and such song schools were the elementary schools of the day. Where there was a town, it is probable that the townsmen and guilds had their own grammar school. The foundations of secular canons, like Chichester, Wells, York, Southwell, Lincoln, Hereford, and Beverley, were more interested in education than the monastic foundations, and they maintained schools, or licensed people to keep them. Generally there was a theological school, under the chancellor, a grammar school, under a master appointed by the chancellor, and a song school under the precentor. On pages 25 and 26 we describe the difference between secular and monastic foundations.

FIG. 12.—A Boy of 1509

There were collegiate churches which carried on the same work, like Winchester and Eton. William of Wykeham founded Winchester, as early as 1382, for "seventy poor and needy scholars, clerks, living collegewise therein and studying and becoming proficient in grammaticals or the art, faculty, or science of grammar." A bird's-eye view of the college is shown in Pl. 7. Wykeham also founded New College, Oxford, and boys went there on leaving Winchester; and they went up at an earlier age than now. Eton came into being in 1440, and Henry VI arranged for it to consist of provost, ten priests, four clerks, six chorister boys, and "twenty-five poor and needy scholars to learn grammar there." The Eton boys of the fifteenth century said the Matins of the Blessed Virgin while making the beds in the dormitories before five o'clock in the morning. King's College, Cambridge, was founded in connection with Eton.

Chantry schools were attached to a church, where the priest taught children, as well as singing Masses for the founder. The chantries were dissolved in 1547.

Grammar schools were sometimes founded in connection

with colleges, as at Queen's College, Oxford, where the boys served as choristers, but had masters of their own and dined in hall with the scholars.

In the Middle Ages the schools taught grammar, logic, and rhetoric, called the Trivium; arithmetic, music, geometry, and astronomy, the Quadrivium; and teaching was mainly oral—this had to be, because, before printing became general, books were far too expensive to be used for class-work. A boy was taught to hold his own in wordy disputation, and to argue on such abstruse questions as—How many angels could sit on a pin's point? We still talk of a Senior Wrangler, and originally this did mean one who could hold his own in disputation. Mediæval education was severely practical; it fitted a man to be a lawyer, but denied him the wider interests which the Renaissance supplied later. The patron saints of schoolboys were St. Katherine of Egypt and St. Nicholas of Myra.

St. Paul's School, founded by Dean Colet for 153 boys, was "for the continuation of a certain school in the cemetery of St. Paul's." The boys were to be taught "All way in good litterature with laten and greke and goode auctours such as have the veray Romayne eliquence joyned withe wysdome, specially Cristyn auctours that wrote theyre wysdome withe clene and chast laten other in verse or in prose." Wolsey founded a school at Ipswich from which boys went up to Christ Church, Oxford. The City Companies played their part, and the Mercers were named as trustees of Dean Colet's School, and the Fishmongers still are for the school at Holt founded by Sir John Gresham in 1555. It is a splendid sign of the sixteenth century that it was held to be a notable thing to found schools, and these were not only for one class. At the sixteenth-century Harrow the scholars were to be of "the poorest sort, if they shall be apt."

Berkhamsted School was founded by another Dean of St. Paul's, John Incent, in 1541, who arranged for "one Free Scole within the towne of Berkhampstedde, of one mete man being a scolemaster, and one other mete man being an ussher for the techyng of children in grammar frely, withoute any exaccion or request of money for the techyng of the same

FIG. 13.—The Old Hall, Berkhamsted School

children." An Elizabethan writer said of the school: "Th'ole building is so strong an faire that the like Grammar Schoole for that point is not to be seene in the whole realme of England"—evidently an enthusiastic old boy. There are large central windows, which mark the hall. On the right hand lived the "one mete man being a scolemaster," as does his successor of to-day; on the left was the house of the "other mete man being an ussher," and probably boys who were boarders lived in their houses.

The interior of the school hall is shown in Fig. 13, and some restoration has been necessary. The hall still remained the central feature of almost any secular building; here the boys were taught, sitting in classes round the room rather like a Sunday school of to-day, and there were not any separate class-rooms. Boys worked long hours, from six till eleven in the morning, and one to six in the afternoon in the summer, and two hours less in the winter. It was not all book work, though; boys and girls were trained in hawking, hunting, archery, and playing upon the lute and virginals as part of their education. One of the school orders at Harrow was: "You shall allow your child at all times bow-shafts, bow-strings, and a bracer (sleeve guard) to exercise shooting."

Holidays were few, and must have seemed far between. At Shrewsbury the boys were allowed eighteen days at Christmas, twelve at Easter, and nine at Whitsuntide.

Roger Ascham was the tutor of Lady Jane Grey and Queen Elizabeth, and must be remembered as one of the first of the great schoolmasters. His book, *The Scholemaster*, published in 1570, marked a great advance in education.

The colleges (Pl. 7) were much like the schools, or for that matter the houses of the period—in fact, the Oxford or Cambridge college of to-day affords an excellent example of the mediæval method of house-planning which obtained up till Elizabeth's time. There was the hall with its screens, the buttery, and kitchen. A chapel was included later, but did not form part of the early mediæval colleges, the students attending the parish church. The hall originally served for common-room as well. All this part of the plan usually occupied one side of a square quadrangle. Around this later were grouped the men's rooms, like the lodgings in an Elizabethan house. College rooms were used by more than one man, as now; the larger as a dormitory for perhaps four men, and the smaller as a study; now the positions are reversed. On the side of the quad opposite the hall came the gatehouse, like the house plan,

FIG. 14.—An Elizabethan Dame School

and here the porter mounted guard, and as an additional precaution the warden's lodging was generally over and around the gateway. Of course all colleges did not follow this plan; there are all sorts of delightful variations of the idea, and skilful adaptations of it to suit the peculiarities of different sites. We hope some of our readers will become architects one of these days, and to such we recommend a reference back to the plan of a Benedictine monastery, Chapter I, Vol. I, and a linking up of this, the inspiration, through the plans of the intervening centuries with the final development in the sixteenth century.

We still talk of Halls and Colleges at Oxford and Cambridge; originally the former were more like hostels for students attending lectures at the University.

A few notes are necessary as to what happened to the cathedrals in the time of Henry VIII. We know boys and girls find the subject confusing.

In Vol. I we described the constitution of a Benedictine monastery, and pointed out how many of those great churches we now call cathedrals were, in pre-Reformation times, the private chapels of the monastery. But if the abbot happened to be a bishop as well, and the church contained his throne, then it became a cathedral. At the dissolution of the monasteries, the monastic cathedral was administered by a chapter of secular canons, and these were said to be of the New Foundation. But during the Middle Ages as well there had been non-monastic cathedrals administered always by secular canons, like Wells, Exeter, and Salisbury, and these were called as of the Old Foundation.

Secular clergy have existed from the earliest times. They were the parish priests, and canons of cathedral and collegiate churches. They lived in the world, had their own houses, and frequently in very early days were married. They did not take the vows of poverty, chastity, and obedience, as the monks did, but agreed, as now, to obey the law of the Church. About the time of the Conquest, at Wells and Exeter the canons began to live in a community and became more like monks, but the custom never became very general.

In the old times the canons were resident. It is this fact which makes Wells Cathedral so interesting, because here we find the bishop's palace, deanery, and houses for the canons and vicars, and far more accommodation than would have been required for a monastic cathedral. Wells is much the same as it was in pre-Reformation days, because it is of the Old Foundation, and was never altered as were so many of the monastic cathedrals in Henry VIII's time, when the monks' quarters were pulled down because they were no longer needed. Canons of the Old Foundation who were not resident appointed vicars to take their place, and these must not be confounded with the minor canons in cathedrals founded by Henry VIII.

There is often confusion between the names canon and prebendary, but in reality they mean the same. A man is canon by reason of being a member of the body of the dean and chapter; prebendary, as holding a certain canonry, or prebend (*præbenda*), or separate estate.

Both Winchester and Eton were founded as collegiate churches, with a chapter, or college, of clergy who made education one of their duties.

Our next illustration (Fig. 15) has been drawn to show a timber-framed house. From the earliest times houses had been

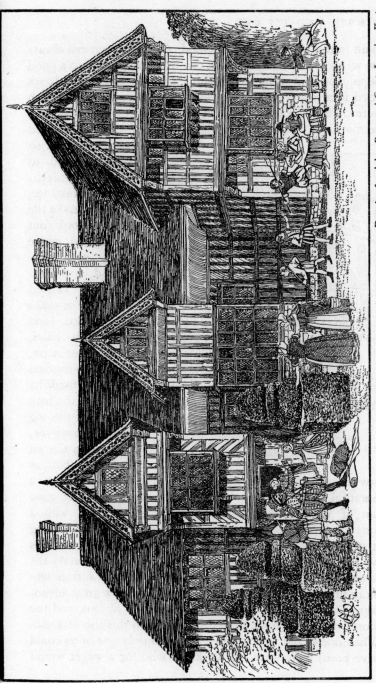

Drawing founded on Rumwood Court, Langley, Kent

Fig. 15.—A Timber-framed House

Sixteenth-Century Stone House, Pl. 9.   Seventeenth-Century House, Pl. 21.   Eighteenth-Century House, Fig. 96.

Eighteenth-Century Town House, Fig. 97

27

built in this way, and such method of construction can always be accepted as evidence that at one time there has been a good supply of timber in the locality. The old workmen always used local materials, and by so doing ensured harmony with surroundings; a house built of local stone, bricks, or timber, seems to fit in and tune with the countryside, and does so because it is so closely related to Mother Earth. Slates, for instance, imported into a tile country look out of key. So where sturdy oaks flourished you find timber-framed houses. The oaks were felled and sawn up by hand. Placed over a pit, a long two-handled saw was used by two men; the man on top of the log was the top sawyer; the one in the pit under, the bottom

Drawn by Sydney R. Jones

FIG. 16.—The framework of a Kentish Timber House

sawyer. Smaller stuff was squared and faced up with a beautiful tool called an adze, which now has nearly gone out of use. In shape it was like a garden hoe, with a longer and sharper blade, and shorter handle. The man using it stood on his work and chopped off thick shavings towards his foot; a skilful craftsmen could face up oak to nearly the same smoothness as with a plane, but the general surface was more undulating and pleasant. This was really a great advantage. The old builders realised that oak was fibrous, and the more you followed the fibre the better, and this the adze did. When one of the writers was a boy (and only one of us could have been) there were old workmen who for a wager would take off one boot, put a penny under the big toe, bring their adze down, and nick the edge of the penny, and not damage the toe. This gives some idea of what dexterous handling of tools can mean.

In building a timber-framed house (Fig. 16), the foundations and two or three courses above the ground were built in masonry to keep the oak away from the damp. On the top of this was laid a sill-piece, into this were framed the uprights, called studs, and the earlier the work is, the closer the studs come together; at the top of the studs was another horizontal sill, and the joists of the floor were rested on the top of this and projected over the framing under. So stage by stage the floors jutted out until the gables were reached, and these again were finished off with overhanging "barge boards"; here the old carpenters enjoyed themselves by inventing beautiful pierced patterns that are almost lace-like in their richness. The roof was sometimes covered with tiles, thatch, or thin stone slabs. The oak studs were filled between with wattle, rather like a hurdle is made now, and then plastered, and this is called wattle-and-daub work, or brick was used for the same purpose, and this is called brick-nogging. The oak was generally left to take on a pleasant grey tint by exposure to the weather, rather like a field gate is now; many half-timbered houses have been ruined in appearance in modern times by being tarred, and the result is altogether too startling and black and white to be pleasant.

Fig. 17 shows a very pleasant old house near Chiddingfold, Surrey. Here the outer walls on the first floor have been covered with tiles, and architects describe this treatment as tile-hanging. In these days the papers are full of complaints against those people who build bungalows, and spoil the appearance of the countryside. If these same people would only go to work like the builders of these old houses did, we should not have so many complaints. If all the old quarries were opened up, and the local brickyards started again, it would help the life of the countryside. What happened in the years before 1914 was that bricks produced by large commercial concerns were used to undersell the products of the smaller brickfields, and then when these had to close down, the brickmakers drifted to the towns to try and find employment; and nobody was much better off, because the price of the imported brick went up, so that it cost just as much, if not more, than the ones the people used to make for themselves.

Pl. 6, of the sixteenth-century barn at Edlesborough, Bucks, should be studied or seen as a magnificent example of old

FIG. 17.—A Tile-hung House, near Chiddingfold, Surrey

carpenters' work. It is ten bays in length, and as each bay is about 16 feet wide, and the width is about 29 feet between the walls, some idea can be gained of the impressiveness of the building. It is, in fact, as beautiful as a cathedral. Nowadays, the corn is stacked in the fields, and the threshing-machine taken to the rick. In the old days it was carted to the barn and stored there, and threshed by flails on a good oak floor by the open door. A flail is described in the eighteenth-century chapter (Fig. 92).

Now as to the kind of life which would have been lived in the old houses we have been describing, and the everyday things they would have used. A good deal of information can

be obtained from old wills, and we give extracts from one
which is extremely interesting. Thomas Quenell, of Lythe
Hill, Chiddingfold, yeoman, died in 1571, and this is how he
disposed of all his possessions: "ffirste, I geve and bequethe
my sowle into the hands of Almightie God my maker and
his sonne Jesu Christe my redeamer throughe whose deathe
and passion I truste to be saved and to
have a gloryous and Joyefull resurrec-
tion emonge the nūber of his electe."

There are various charitable bequests,
but the main interest to us is the description given of the various parts of
Thomas's house and the careful provision he made for the comfort of
his wife Agnys; thus; "Itm̄, I geve
and bequethe to Agnys my wyfe
enduringe the tyme of her naturall lyfe
my parler in the weste syde of my
house at Lythehill wᶜh adioynethe to
the hawle there, the chamber over the
same pler, the garret above the same
chamber, the lofte over the hawle and
the kytchen lofte wᵗh free ingres,
egress and regres. Roome and fyer in
the said hawle at all tymes and also
halfe the kytchen, and fyer boote (fire-
wood) to dresse meate and drinke,
bake and brewe, and to doe all other
necessaryes mete and convenyent in the

FIG. 18.—Physician,
1562

same kytchen at all tymes and halfe the newe coope nowe
standinge in the sayde kytchen."

Agnys as well was to have "all my oulde stable wᶜh
adioynethe to the weste syde of my house, the weste ende of
my Raynge (barn or granary) to laye haye or strawe in, and
halfe the rest of my Raynge, and also the upper gates for her
cattayles." The will is thus of great interest because it mentions
the surroundings of the house. Agnys also had "all my herber
(garden) wᶜh adioynethe to the easte syde of my saide house.
And all my orcharde wᶜh adioynethe to the sayde herber on

the sowethe syde of my sayde house from the newe pale that adioynethe unto the sayde herber on the easte syde unto the home felde on the weste syde and extendethe from the sayde house on the northe syde unto the lyttle meade on the sowethe syde." The plan, Fig. 21, will help to explain all this. When Agyns dies it is all to revert to Robert, a brother, the heir, and who is to share the house with Agnys. She has a good deal of land left to her in other places, and a barn is mentioned, but for this she had to pay a rent to Robert. Thomas leaves

FIG. 19.—Children of 1563

to "Elynor Qwennell my cossyn twoe eweshipe," and £51 13s. 4d. to be paid "to her at the daye of her maryage. And I will that she contynue until the tyme of her marriage in service wth Agnys my wife."

Robert Page, a servant, has one cow and £6 14s. 4d.; Willm Wodier, another servant, "one hecforde (heifer) bullocke; Willm Allyn three ewe teggs; Agnys Todman one hecforde bullocke." Brothers and a brother-in-law are remembered, and "I geve to eűy one of my godchildren xijd. (12d.) that will requyre to have the same." Then the will goes back to Agnys, the wife, who is to have "Sixe of my beste keene (except one cowe named Lustye) fower hecforde wherof one blacke wth a whitte sterre in the forhed, one Redde wyth a whitte backe one other Redde wth a chynned (narrow strip of white) face and one browne wth a whitte face." She had as well "six of my best oxen wth yokes and chaynes meete for them my newe wollen wheles my yonge baye Amblynge mare my blacke Amblynge mare wth a whitte steare in the forhed twoe steares nowe goynge in Anstrode the one havinge a brended (brindled) face and the other being a vallowe steare wth a whitte face." Agnys in addition had two other heifers, twelve ewes, twelve lambs, "my fyve hoggꝗ of one sorte beinge aboute twoe yeares oulde at Michaelmas laste, twoe Redde hogge goyne emonge my wylde hogges," and half the wheat, rye, and oats growing, and one acre of grass Thomas had bought and which was "to be mowen made and caryed awaye wᵗhin fortenighte after mydsomer nexte." Thomas left to his wife "all my poultrey whatsoever my three beste beddes wᵗh boulsters pyllowes and pyllowe coate belonging to them my beste bedstedle (excepte one) all my sheatꝗ (excepte three payer of canvas sheatꝗ) all my beste blancketꝗ (except one payer) my three best coverlette and one Qwylte all my pewter vessyll, (except fyve pewter platters twoe pewter disshes and one basone wᶜh were my fathers) my beste and my leaste twoe candlestyckꝗ my beste

brasse potts, my beste and my leaste twoe kettles, and my kettle wᶜh was bounde wᵗh yron by Hewghe the Smythe, my posnet [a little pot] of belle brasse, my leaste Skyllet [pot with long handle, see Fig. 20] of brasse, and the occupačon

FIG. 20.—"My leaste Skyllet"

of my Cawdron as often as she shall have nede, so long tyme as she shall be dwellinge at Lyethehill aforsayde and also halfe of almanꝗ of my wodden vessill to be equally divyded (excepte my beste vate and my best kyfe) [tub used in brewing]."

Thomas left to his wife "halfe my bakon at the beame (excepte the twoe greateste flytches and the twoe leaste flytches) halfe my Larde and greace, twoe of the beste flytches of dryed beefe, twoe of my beste table clothes, twoe of my beste towels, halfe of all my table napkyns, one dozen of my beste spons, my three beste soup cuppes, the beste cheste wᶜh I nowe have to my selfe, and all the resedue of my cofers (except the beste of them) wᶜh coferys nowe ys in the tenure of my sayd wyfe. The Resedewe of all my goodꝗ cattayls and chattayls moveables and ummoveables"—went to Robert, the brother.

The interest of all this is, that not only do we get an excellent idea of the house and its surroundings, but also of its contents, and one feels the better for knowing the name of that Elizabethan cow "Lustye." Lythe Hill still stands on the road from Haslemere to Anstead Brook, but alteration has made the house not so suitable for illustration as the one we have selected, Fig. 17.

The plan, Fig. 21, in conjunction with the sketch of the exterior of the house will explain the position of the rooms. The hall was as high as the ground and first floors at the two ends, so this meant two separate staircases to get to the two chambers—probably Robert the heir had the one over the kitchen. The servants would have slept in the garrets, and we saw the beginning of this practice in the fifteenth century.

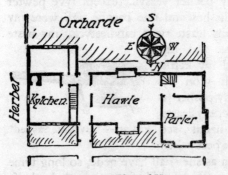

FIG. 21.—Plan of House

The plan is of interest as showing that with the simpler country folk the old mediæval type of arrangement was still adhered to; this can be seen by reference to the houses in Vol. I. At the same time, if this plan had been extended on the left hand by a buttery and winter parlour, it would have developed into the ⊓ type of plan—a form said to have been adopted as complimentary to Elizabeth. Whole families were used to living together in those days, and it enabled them to have one fine house instead of many small ones. Erasmus wrote to a friend: "More hath built neare London, upon the Thames side, a commodious house, neither meane nor subject to envie, yet magnificent enough; there he converseth affably with his family, his wife, his son and daughter-in-lawe, his three daughters and their husbands, with eleven grandchildren."

It is unlikely that the vanished Beaufort House at Chelsea shown in Pl. 8 was the one More built; but it is of the style of his period or a little later, and gives an idea of the kind of gardens which surrounded the dwellings of the time, and which had altered but little in style when this engraving was made.

Agnys seems to have had the larger share of the house, and poor Robert could only have had the chamber over the kitchen; he added a wing to the house later, but as he died in 1612, forty-one years after Thomas, he may have been unmarried when he succeeded. It is also very evident that Agnys intended to carry on farming operations on her own account.

The bequests of cattle and stock to servants are of interest, as showing that these men must have had holdings of land of their own, on which they could feed the beasts left to them by Thomas in his will; a farm labourer to-day would be rather embarrassed by a cow or even "one hecforde bullocke."

It may be as well to try to explain this. In Vol. I we spoke of the mediæval system of land-holding, which we will now summarise, because it is very essential to understand this if we are to appreciate the change which came over England in the sixteenth century.

In a typical manor of the Middle Ages, the lord retained perhaps one-third of the land for his own use, and this was called the demesne, but it was not enclosed or fenced off, and it formed part of the arable land on which crops were grown; the remainder was divided between the villeins, and farmed by them for the common benefit. They shared the hay grown on the meadows, and their pigs under the charge of the swine-herds fed on the acorns in the woodlands. The villagers paid for their share of the common fields by working for the lord on the demesne land for two or three days in the week, and they sometimes paid a little in kind, like eggs, or fowls, with the further obligation that they followed their lord to war.

This method of farming was called the open field system, and did not altogether die out in England until the end of the eighteenth century.

The enclosures of which we hear so much started with the demesne land, and two causes contributed to this. These were the scarcity of labour caused by the Black Death of 1348, and the fact that it was more profitable to keep sheep, and sell wool, than grow corn. The lord often withdrew his demesne lands in the common fields, and put them down to pasture; this helped at first, because less labour was required to tend sheep than to grow corn, and the waste lands were enclosed for the same purpose. Later on, however, as the population increased, this became a great hardship, and men could not find work to do. In Vol. I we saw how some of the land-owners who could not get men to work their land, as villeins, started letting it on stock and land leases, and charged a rent; from this class the yeomen developed, and judging by the number of small houses they built in the fifteenth and sixteenth centuries, they must have been prosperous then. But in the sixteenth century an altogether different spirit was introduced into land-holding. In the Middle Ages land was held to produce food, and to guarantee a supply of sturdy men-at-arms; at the dissolution of the monasteries nearly one fifteenth part of England changed hands, and the new landlords were a greedy, rapacious lot, who wanted to make things pay. Under the old system the land was worked for the common good; the new method allowed the pushing man to forge ahead, often at the expense of his fellows.

FIG. 22.—A Water Carrier

Sir Thomas More, one of the best Englishmen who ever lived, published his celebrated book *Utopia* in 1516, and in it he says of the land enclosers: "The husbandmen be thrust oute of their owne, or els either by coveyne and fraude, or by violent oppression they be put besydes it, or by wronges and injuries thei be so weried, that they be compelled to sell all: by one meanes therfore or by other, either by hooke or crooke they must needes departe awaye, poore, selye, wretched soules." Till the beginning of the sixteenth century the monks

PLATE 7

PLATE 8

Engraving by Kip

Beaufort House by the Thames at Chelsea, *c*.1585, now destroyed

had given alms, looked after sick and needy folk, and enter-
tained travellers. At the suppression of the monasteries a very
large number of people found themselves homeless, and this
happened at a time when the number of men employed on
the farms was being reduced by enclosures and sheep-keeping;
so a very miserable state of affairs came about. Laws were
passed to make men work, but there was not any to do;
vagabonds were whipped and put in the stocks. The Tudors did
their best to remedy matters; more laws were passed that no
one must hold more than one farm, or keep more than 2000
sheep; that crops must be grown, buildings repaired, and men
employed. It was not, however, until the middle of Elizabeth's
reign that things improved. Then meat and corn began to
fetch a better price, and that of wool declined, and this made
the growing of crops and keeping of cattle profitable, and
gave more employment.

Fitzherbert published his book in 1523, and this marked
an advance in the art of agriculture.

While writing about country life we may as well include
another of the drawings we have made to show the development of the windmill, though as this has been drawn from
a mill which is still existing it should not be taken as typical
of the sixteenth century. In Vol. I, Chapter IV, an illustration
was given of a post mill, so called because the whole structure
was balanced and turned on a great oak post set up and
securely strutted. In this type, if the wind changed, the mill
had to be turned round on its post by hand, until the main
sails came into the wind; as this was very hard work, the
millwright hit upon an ingenious labour-saving contrivance.
This is shown in Fig. 23, and consisted of a vane set up on
the end of the long fantail, or steps at the back of the mill.
This vane did not operate while the main sails were in the
wind, but if the latter changed and came from the side, the
vane came into action, and its spindle, by means of bevel
gears, turned the vertical shafting on the left, and this latter
by more gears moved the carriage supporting the fantail
around a circular track. Remember, the whole mill above the
circular round house turned on its central post, so that as it
was moved by the action of the vane, the main sails would

FIG. 23.—A Post Mill

Smock Mill, Fig. 75.   Tower Mill, Fig. 93.   Handmill, Fig. 94

come into the wind, and then the vane would be out of it, and so stop. The iron wheel and chain hanging from the above balcony operated a spindle through the main shaft, which opened and shut the louvres on the sails. The little balcony is a very pleasant piece of design, and the shoot for sacks at the side of the steps should be noticed.

The Tudors were great gardeners and fond of flowers, and their houses were set about with herbers and pleasant courts. There was a fore-court in front, and a base-court around which were grouped the stables and offices. A terrace against the house overlooked the gardens and parterre. The flower beds were edged with rosemary, lavender, marjoram, and thyme. Fig. 24 shows a delightful little garden, still existing at Hampton Court, which dates from the days of Henry VIII. Here that monarch may have walked with Anne Boleyn and the ladies of her Court. This type is called a formal garden, and the design probably came down from mediæval times. In the early days, people had to wall in their houses, castles, and monasteries for security, and even when this necessity had passed, the feeling remained that any garth, or garden, needed a wall, or hedge, as a frame. This meant a certain formality in design; paths were straight, yews were cut into quaint shapes, called topiary work, and mazes and labyrinths were popular. It was all very rational, because a house must have a certain square hardness about it, and looks bare if placed in a forest glade: a garden is the clothing of a house, and should be designed; so the effect is lost if the garden itself is a rather bad imitation of Nature. Gardens and gardening became a very vital part of Tudor lives. With greater opportunities for peaceful travel, many new and interesting plants and trees were brought home from abroad. Red and black currants were introduced from Europe and so called because they were supposed to have been small grapes; really they are of the gooseberry family. Thomas Cromwell planted rhubarb for medicinal purposes, and apricots, oranges and other hot-weather fruits had become well known. William Harrison had 300 varieties of simples in his garden, and the great herbalist Gerard had a physic garden in Holborn which included upward of 1000 different kinds of plants.

FIG. 24.—A Tudor Garden, at Hampton Court

Here is a description of a Tudor garden: "It is so encompassed with parks full of deer, delicious gardens, groves ornamented with trellis work, cabinets of verdure, and walks, that it seems to be a place pitched upon by pleasure herself to dwell in along with health. In the pleasure and artificial gardens are many columns and pyramids of marble, two fountains that spout water, one round, the other like a pyramid upon which are perched small birds that stream water out of their bills. There is, besides, another pyramid of marble full

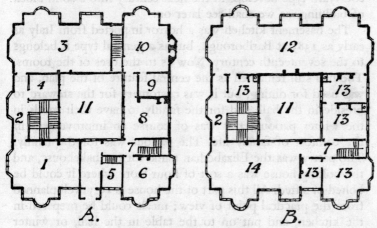

FIG. 25.—Plan of House

of concealed pipes, which spirt upon all who come within their reach." These hydraulic jokes appealed to the Tudors, and they loved flowers.

From gardens we pass to houses.

Our illustration (Fig. 25) is the plan of one of the larger houses, such as were built by the more considerable land-owners at the end of Elizabeth's reign. A on the left-hand side shows the ground floor, raised up sufficiently to have cellars under. The entrance is by way of the screens, into the hall at 1. The principal staircase is at 2, and the parlour 3 has a smaller room off it at 4. At 5 is the buttery, with the winter parlour at 6, back stairs 7, kitchen 8, pastry 10, with the bolting-house off it at 9, and 11 is the inner court. B is the first floor, access to which is gained by the staircases 2 and 7; 12 is the gallery, 14 the great chamber, and 13 the bedrooms. It will be noticed that the type of plan follows in many ways that of the fifteenth-century house shown in Vol. I, Chapter IV. The hall, winter parlour, and kitchen offices come in much the same position, but the house has better accommodation, planned in a more compact way. The types seem to have been like this one, with the rooms arranged round an inner court, or spread out like an ⊓ or Н. The more compact courtyard type develops in the next century into a solid block of building, as we shall see later on.

The basement kitchen was a horror imported from Italy as early as 1583 at Barlborough, but as a general type it belongs to the seventeenth century. Now as to the uses of the rooms. The hall still remained as the central feature of the plan, and was used for dining, but it was customary for the steward to preside in the hall, and for the family to have their meals in the winter parlour; this was of course an improvement in the comfort of family life. The parlour was for the family. The pastry was the Elizabethan name for the bakehouse, and the bolting-house was a sort of flour store where it could be bolted or sifted. All this part of the house is very well planned from the practical point of view; meals could be prepared in the kitchen, and put on to the table in the hall, or winter parlour, without being chilled by journeys through long passages, as came to be the case in the next century. And in the Tudor House, kitchen and cooking was of the uttermost importance. Meals were large and very elaborate. Gentry usually dined at eleven, and the meal often occupied three hours, and supped about six o'clock. Merchants and farmers dined at noon, and supped at seven or eight. Breakfast was usually taken as an early snack. Meat eating was excessive, though fish was beginning to come more into fashion among the upper classes, although Thomas Tusser writes:

> "Good ploughman look weekly of Custom and right,
> For roast meat on Sundays, Thursdays at night."

The usual meal partaken in a labourer's cottage would probably consist of bread (with an admixture of rye in it), bacon, milk, curds and perhaps beer or cider. Brawn was a favourite dish among all classes—hogs were specially bred for the purpose.

The store cupboard in a large home was always well filled, for we must remember that the housewife had to be ready for any influx of visitors without having recourse to shops (especially in the country) as we do to-day. Hence we read of the salting down of barrels of fish, meat, and in the store cupboard of pepper, mace, cloves, ginger, figs, raisins, hops, honey, oil, vinegar, salt, almonds, dates, saffron and cinnamon, and many other stores. There is not room to enumerate. Pastries and cakes were made and jellies of all colours. Stale ale (or ale a year old) and strong beer, also metheglin, cider, and perry were conserved in large quantities as well as fifty-six different sorts of wine.

Roasting was still done on the spit and baking either in iron boxes placed in the fire, or in the brick oven at the side of the fireplace. No china was as yet used. Wooden platters and drinking vessels for the poor, now being replaced gradually by pewter, and by silver in the richer houses and also by glass from Venice, and by delft ware from Holland. A rough English pottery had long been made, and this was used as Harrison says, "pots of earth of sundry colours and moulds many with pewter rims."

We saw in the thirteenth, fourteenth, and fifteenth centuries how the lord's solar was always upstairs. The habit continued in the sixteenth century, and the great chamber at 14 answers to our drawing-room. In the house of a noble it would have been called the presence chamber, but it might have had a bed in it. There is a picture in the National Gallery by Gerard Terbosch, a seventeenth-century painter, called "The Guitar Lesson"; a lady is playing, and there is the music master and another friend. In the corner of the room is shown a typical seventeenth-century bed. This again was a survival of the time when the solar was parlour, presence chamber, and bedroom all rolled into one. The long gallery at 12 is another typical feature of Elizabethan and Jacobean plans; often of great length, this must have made a delightful addition to a house, and formed a splendid place for romps and games, or the display of pictures and fine furniture. There were now many more bedrooms, and good attics for the servants, but there was still an absence of passages, and one room often led to another.

The illustration (Pl. 9) is of the exterior of the house, and it will be apparent at once that some very considerable change has come over the spirit of design. This house is different from those of the thirteenth, fourteenth, and fifteenth centuries, which were all closely related. This illustration shows the beginning of Renaissance design, or rebirth of the old classical forms of architecture.

We have seen how, at the fall of Constantinople in 1453, the scholars who fled from that city spread the knowledge of classical literature and architecture, but the designers in Italy had not so much to learn from this source as in the northern countries. This came about because of the many buildings remaining of old Roman times, and Gothic architecture never obtained the hold in Italy, or was quite the same as in England, for example. Boys and girls who later on see Siena and Orvieto Cathedrals will realise this.

The Renaissance movement had started earlier in Italy.

Filippo Brunelleschi (1377-1446), fired by the classical tradition, was the first of the Italian architects to work in the new manner, and the Pazzi Chapel in Florence was built early in the fifteenth century. Donatello the sculptor was born 1386, died 1466, and then followed the other giants of the fifteenth century, Luca Della Robbia, Botticelli, Leonardo da Vinci, Michelangelo, Titian, and Holbein, who was born 1497, and died 1543. Nature was prodigal with genius in the fifteenth century, and these men gave to the Renaissance every beauty of form, colour, and shape that was conceivable. In the end it filtered into England, and it was the tomb which Henry the Eighth put up to his father in Westminster Abbey which first made Englishmen familiar with the new style. Perhaps this is what makes the Abbey so very wonderful. We can see here in Henry III's work the Gothic at its finest period; in Henry VII's Chapel its culmination in the exquisite fan vaulting to the roof, and in his tomb the beginning of the Renaissance. A drawing of this latter is given in Fig. 1 in the Introduction.

PLATE 7

Fritwell House, Oxfordshire, Sixteenth Century

Timber-framed House, Fig. 15. Seventeenth-Century House, Fig. 56, Pl. 22. Eighteenth-Century House, Pl. 29, Fig. 96. Eighteenth-Century Town House, Fig. 97.

PLATE 10

The "Job" Room at Bradninch, Devon, showing the Interior Porch. Late Sixteenth Century

Seventeenth-Century Interiors, Fig. 58, Pl. 27.   Eighteenth-Century Interiors, Figs. 99, 121, Pl. 28

Our book seems full of long explanations, and we apologise; yet we are so anxious to impress upon our readers this fact of growth, flower, decay, and rebirth that we risk seeming tedious if we can establish this principle.

Our illustration (Pl. 9) shows that the Elizabethan house was more symmetrical than that of the fifteenth century; the various parts are as exactly balanced as possible. The hall, which was expressed outside by a roof of its own in the century before, now forms part of the house and cannot be distinguished from the outside. The four-centred arches have gone, and the only one that appears is semicircular in shape. The windows have square heads, with label moulds typical of earlier times, and, like the gables, are still Gothic in character. There was so much more window in these times than formerly that we can understand the complaint in one of Lord Bacon's essays: "You shall have sometimes fair houses so full of glass, that one cannot tell where to be come, to be out of the sun or cold." The people of the time said of a famous Derbyshire house, "Hardwick Hall, more glass than wall." At Montacute, 1580, is cut over the door: "Through this wide opening gate, none come too early—none return too late."

The Elizabethans were rather like the men of Romanesque times, in that they produced an architecture which was amazingly picturesque, and fashioned out of the Gothic tradition and what they could pick up of the new Italian fashion. The work was full of vigour; later on, as the designers came to know more, they produced work with less life about it.

Another development in the sixteenth century which is of great interest was the wooden staircase. In Vol. I we saw how the people were satisfied, right through the Middle Ages, with circular stone staircases like those in church towers, and one of these was illustrated in Chapter I. Sometimes the same form was used in oak, the solid treads being tenoned into a centre newel; then quite suddenly, in the sixteenth century, beautiful staircases like the one illustrated here, Fig. 26, began to be made, and from this time on we shall find infinite variety of design, and beautiful workmanship, used in this part of

Founded on staircase at The Charterhouse, London

FIG. 26.—Sixteenth-Century Staircase

Seventeenth-Century Stair, Fig. 59.   Eighteenth-Century Stair, Fig. 100

the house. The same name of newel is given to the square terminal posts; into these were framed the strings, which support the ends of the treads and risers to the stairs. The handrail, again, is framed into the newels, and between string and handrail comes the balustrade, formed either with separate balusters, or the beautiful arcaded treatment shown in our sketch.

The Elizabethan builders were great men for beautiful woodwork, and they had at their disposal splendid craftsmen. The fifteenth century was the great period for church wood-work, and many of the beautiful screens, choir stalls, and pulpits now remaining were made then. This work had trained up a splendid school of "joyners," as they were called, so that in the sixteenth century this trade was one with fine traditions behind it. They seized on the Renaissance detail, and really ran riot with it, but notwithstanding all this, the results they obtained were surprisingly fine. Pl. 10 illustrates an Elizabethan parlour, and shows walls panelled with oak, and a modelled plaster ceiling. The internal porch to the room is a very typical and beautiful feature, which must have added to comfort. The rich elaboration of these interiors may be seen in the plates of Nash's *Mansions*, and in some of the rooms now set up in the Victoria and Albert Museum, such as that from Sizergh, Westmorland, where the panelling is inlaid; there is another fine room at Chastleton, Oxfordshire. The plaster frieze was often painted in gay colours, as at Boughton Malherbe rectory, Kent, and sometimes the windows were filled with fine heraldic stained glass, as at Ockwells, Berkshire, and the great parlour at Gilling Castle, Yorkshire, perhaps the most splendid typical interior of all. We illustrate one piece (Pl. 11); it is dated 1585 and signed below the two cupids by Bernard Dininckhoff, the Dutch craftsman who designed and carried it out.

The furniture was substantial, but still scarce, and a writer of 1585 says:

"The Royal treasures in furniture and tapestries are kept only in that palace, in which for the time being the Queen resides, and when she moves to another, everything is taken away, only the bare walls are left standing."

Presses date from early days; these were wardrobes hanging or shelved in which clothes were put; also cupboards, formerly cup-boards (shelves or boards on which were kept the drinking vessels), were by now enclosed and became the livery cupboard, containing the wages in kind or "livery" of the servants, bread, butter, cheese, candles, etc., and the court cupboard containing dry goods belonging to the master or mistress.

Sideboards came into fashion in Elizabeth's time, solely for the display of plate. Nests of oak boxes were sometimes placed in the cupboards and chests as a way of storing goods tidily, but it was not until the seventeenth century that these boxes were placed on runners and became a chest of drawers. Chairs were still few and in an inventory of a house with thirty rooms only nineteen chairs were found. Stools and chests took their place as seats. Opinions differ as to the date of upholstery, but as a rule, except for the ceremonial X-type, chairs (Pl. 13) are usually found with loose cushions only.

Tables, of trestle shape in the Middle Ages (Pl. 12), are now framed, though still generally heavy and cumbersome (Pl. 12). Mirrors of glass, save for a few rare Venetian ones, are unknown. Henry VIII used toilet mirrors of burnished metal and crystal.

No English pile carpet has been found prior to 1570, but many beautiful Oriental examples were brought into the country. Englishwomen worked carpets in tapestry, embroidery, and petit-point. These "carpets" were more often hung on the walls and put over the tables than on the floor, and rushes, either loose or plaited into a flat covering, were general on the floors.

What a curious practice of early Tudor days according to our ideas, with little to recommend it, and some emphatic drawbacks! If, as is possible, the rushes were allowed to accumulate, they must have been ideal breeding grounds for horrid insects. This is confirmed by Tusser's artless but apposite advice:

> "While wormwood hath seed, get a bundle or twain
> To save against March, to make flea to refrain
> Where Chamber is swept and that wormwood is strown,
> No flea for his life dare abide to be known."

PLATE 11

Painted Glass, 1585
From Gilling Castle, Yorkshire
By Bernard Dininckhoff

PLATE 12

A Linenfold Pattern Chest

Table and Benches at Lyddington Bede-house, Rutland

Bulbous Leg Table, now the Communion Table at Blyford, Suffolk

Seventeenth-Century Furniture, Fig. 60, Pl. 28. Eighteenth-Century Furniture, Figs. 101-7

PLATE 13

Enclosed Arm-chair, latter half of

Queen Mary Tudor's Chair, Winchester Cathedral,

He at least assumes the regularity of sweeping, but in his most
savagely unfavourable report on the subject, Erasmus suggests
that the decaying heaps were the repository of all sorts of
filth, and remained uncleared for twenty years, with results
decidedly detrimental to health. But possibly the great scholar
was exceptionally unfortunate in his experiences, and his
chronic weak health and disappointments may have made him
peevish and inclined to exaggerate. He writes, however, with
great appreciation of the charm of the English girls, and their
delightful way of kissing the guest on arrival and leaving.

Another Dutch visitor, a medical man called Levine Lemnie,
paints about half a century later a very much brighter and
more attractive picture, which we quote; matters must have
improved vastly in the interval, even allowing for the personal
equation. He remarks: "And besides this, the neat cleanliness
the exquisite finenesse, the pleasaunte and delightful furniture
in every poynte for household, wonderfully rejoysed me; their
chambers and parlours strawed over with sweete herbs
refreshed me; their nosegayes finely entermingled with sundry
sorte of fragraunte floures in their bedchambers and privy
rooms, with comfortable smell cheered me up and entirely
delighted all my senses" (*The Touchstone of Complexion*, 1576).

Contemporary writers speak much of the increased wealth
and luxury of the country, one while noting three improvements: the multitude of "chimneys" (fireplaces) lately erected,
feather beds instead of straw pallets, and vessels of wood now
giving place to pewter, adds, "Even many farmers also have
learned to garnish their cupboards with plate, their joined
beds with tapestry and silk hangings, and their tables with
carpets (worked tablecloths) and fine napery, whereby the
wealth of country doth appear." William Harrison, however,
has his doubts as to the improvements made and he writes:
"In times past men were contented to dwell in houses built
of sallow, willow, plumtree, hardbeam and elm, so that the
use of oak was in manner dedicated wholly unto churches,
religious houses, prince's palaces, noblemen's lodgings, and
navigation; but now all these are rejected, and nothing but
oak any whit regarded. And yet see the change! For when
our houses were built of willow, then had we oaken men; but

FIG. 27.—Sixteenth-Century Bed

Seventeenth-Century Bed, Fig. 60.   Eighteenth-Century Bed, Fig. 107

now that our houses are come to be made of oak, our men
are not only become willow, but a great many, through Persian
delicacy crept in among us, altogether of straw: which is a
sore alteration.   In those the courage of the owner was a
sufficient defence to keep the house in safety, but now the
assurance of the timber, double locks and bolts, must defend
the man from robbing. Now have we many chimneys (fireplaces); and yet our tenderlings complain of rheums, catarrhs,

50

and poses. Then had we none but reredosses [movable backs to the fires] and our heads did never ache. For as the smoke in those days was supposed to be a sufficient hardening for the timbers of the house, so it was reported a far better medicine to keep the good man and his family from the quake or pose, wherewith as then very few were oft acquainted."

Fig. 27 is of an Elizabethan bed, and here again is a riot of carving which hardly leaves a square inch of wood unfretted; yet the result is very beautiful. It is amusingly Classic, and the bedposts are turned into very free translations of one of the orders, this time the Ionic. The bedspread, curtains, and valance to the tester would all have been embroidered by hand. We noted in talking of the plan of the bedrooms how often these were passage rooms, one leading through to another. This was doubtless one of the reasons for the four posts and curtains, and the large size of the beds. One could draw the curtains, and make the bed into the bedroom. These beds were thought a great deal of, and treasured; in the old will we have drawn on, we see how beds are often left as legacies to friends and relations.

The next illustration (Fig. 28) has been drawn from the Hall of the Middle Temple in London, which dates from 1570. It has been badly damaged by German bombs, and the very elaborately carved entrance screen smashed, but it has escaped actual destruction. The roof is a very splendid example of double hammer-beam design, and marks the final development of that type. We saw in the fifteenth century how this method of construction was arrived at. In Vol. I we described the uses of the various parts of the roof. Here we get the principal rafters, which are not visible but occur at each bay, whose hammer-beams, two on each side, come under principals and are supported by curved braces. Above these comes a collar-beam with an arched brace under it. The purlins are framed in between the principals, and under these again are arched braces which go from hammer-beam to hammer-beam. Now the details and mouldings of this roof are Renaissance in character, but its form is Gothic, and after these days the timbered roof disappears, with all its play of light and shade, and suggestion of mystery and gloom, and we shall find either flat ceilings or

Founded on the Middle Temple Hall, London

FIG. 28.—Elizabethan Hall, Sixteenth Century

Seventeenth-Century Saloon, Pl. 22. Eighteenth-Century Hall, Fig. 99

plaster vaults. The windows as well retain a little of the Gothic character. The screen at the end was a splendid specimen of Elizabethan woodwork, with woodwork a century later round the openings.

Now as to the life led in the larger houses.

Through all the ages people have amused themselves by playing on musical instruments. Quite at the beginning of things, some cheerful old savage, in aiming a blow at a friend, may have hit an old hollow log instead, and noticed that it gave out a pleasant note. Interested, he repeated the performance, and found that blows of varying strength, on different materials, gave him a range of several notes. Or perhaps he listened to the woodpecker. In some such way one could trace the development of the harmonica, with its graded wood or metal bars, and all the range of instruments like drums, gongs, cymbals, triangles, and tambourines, which produce pleasant noises rather than tuneful notes. Or the early musician, sewing up a skin with the intestines of an animal, found that they were tuneful when dry and stretched, or noticed that the twang

FIG. 29.—Henry VIII playing a Harp

of his bowstring was musical; we might look to some such source for the beginning of the harp, monochord, viol, psaltery, dulcimer, spinet, and piano. The origin of the wind instruments is easily guessed: the horns of animals must have led the way to pipes and flutes, bugles and trumpets, and the noble organ. When Joshua besieged Jericho he was commanded that "seven priests shall bear before the ark seven trumpets of rams' horns."

Illustration Fig. 29 shows Henry VIII playing a harp, and the harp is shown because it can be taken as the forerunner of the modern piano. When girls of to-day play on the piano, by means of a very complicated bit of machinery, they strike the strings with little hammers, instead of plucking them with their fingers. One would have thought that in musical instruments men would have been content with the simplest apparatus, but very little experience is necessary for us to find out that, even in the production of music, man has striven for mechanism to help him.

It may be helpful if we give a description of some of the different sorts of musical instruments used in the old days, and show their connection with those of to-day. The monochord was in use as early as the twelfth century. It had only one string, with a movable bridge, and was plucked by the finger. A bow was sometimes used on it. The organistrum, or symphony, was a development of the monochord. A rosined wheel was placed under the string, and turned by a handle at one end. It was called as well the vielle à roue, or viol with a wheel, or vielle. Little stops at the side were either turned, pulled out, or pressed in, to stop off the strings, just as one does with a violin, and the rosined wheel was the mechanical equivalent of the rosined bow. The hurdy-gurdy, which is still sometimes seen being played in the streets, is the lineal descendant of the organistrum. It was an aristocratic instrument in the eighteenth century, but could never have been anything but dismal. Boys and girls who learn Greek have words pointed out to them which by wonderful sound carry their meaning. Here is an English one, hurdy-gurdy, which does the same.

The manichord of the thirteenth century was the first stringed instrument to be played from a keyboard. The clavichord started as early as the end of the fourteenth century, and did not reach its highest development until the beginning of the eighteenth century. It had a very simple keyboard; the finger struck one end of a balanced lever, at the other end of which was a brass pin called a tangent. This not only struck the string, but stopped off the length which determined the note, and two or three notes were made on the same string, by different tangents striking at different lengths. Later, each note had its separate string, so it was an elementary piano because the difference between that instrument and the spinet, or harpsichord, was that in the former the strings were struck by hammers (invented in 1709 by a Florentine), in the latter plucked by a metal point, leather spine, or quill, on what is called a jack. The clavi-cymbal, virginal, and clavecin were all played in this way.

Fig. 30 shows a clavicytherium, or upright spinet of the sixteenth century. Its likeness to a harp is at once apparent. The fingers strike on to a balanced lever, which, by an inge-nious contrivance, pushes a jack with a leather spine on it through the back-board, and plucks the string. Its com-pass was about the same as the human voice. We shall see later how the next development was to put the clavicy-therium flat on its back, and then after

FIG. 30.—Clavicytherium

Spinet, Fig. 62.   Piano, Fig. 109

a re-arrangement of the keyboard it is called the spinet, or harpsichord.

The dulcimer was another forerunner of the piano, and consisted of a sounding-board across which strings of varying lengths were stretched, and struck by hammers. Pepys went to a puppet play in Covent Garden, on May 14, 1662, and wrote in his diary: "Here, among the fiddles, I first saw a dulcimer played on with sticks, knocking of the strings, and is very pretty." The psaltery had the same form as the dulcimer, but was played by plucking the strings.

Many other musical instruments are named by old writers. The viol was like a violin, but with a flat back, and pieces of gut across the finger-board; it was played with a bow. Viola-da-gamba was played while held between the knees. Sir Toby Belch says of Sir Andrew Aguecheek, "He plays o' the viol-de-gamboys." The lute was the forerunner of the mandoline, but had a rather pear-shaped body; the treble lute had a bent head to take less room, archlutes were very big ones. The theorbo was lute-shaped and large, the cittern was lute-shaped and small. The gittern was a lute with a fiddle-shaped body, the guitar one with a flat back. All these instruments were plucked with a plectrum. The rebec was a three-stringed fiddle.

Of the wind instruments, of course the organ is quite the most wonderful, and has ages of history behind it. In mediæval times we read of the organ portative; this was a small pipe organ which was carried by a strap over the shoulder, and played with the right hand, while the left worked the bellows. The positive organ remained in one place, and was not carried about. The regal was a sort of harmonium, with bellows behind the keyboard like large flat books. The clarion was a trumpet, the shawm and pomme were whistle flutes with rather bell-shaped ends. The hautboy was the successor to the shawm. Recorders were whistle flutes; the hornpipe had a horn added to the end of a pipe. Cromhorns, like whistle flutes with ends on a curved line. The penny whistle is a blood relation to the stately organ, which in reality is many whistles played in a mechanical way; here we must confess that man, if he made a horrible failure of the hurdy-gurdy, achieved splendid success with the organ.

A number of these instruments could, of course, be combined into an orchestra, as we see in Pl. 2, where a concert is being given by nine performers on six different instruments. Three people who are not playing are unlikely to be vocalists, for full orchestral pieces were usually quite separate from singing numbers. Girls and boys will wonder if they could have enjoyed the performance, but it is possible sometimes

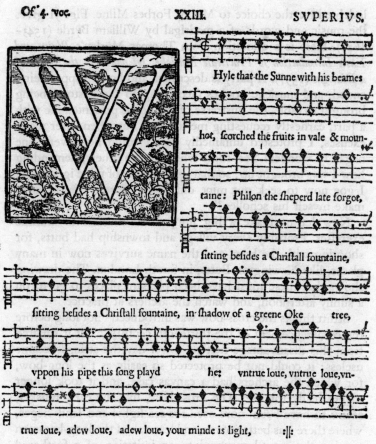

Of 4. voc.   XXIII.   SVPERIVS.

Hyle that the Sunne with his beames

hot, scorched the fruits in vale & moun-

taine: Philon the sheperd late forgot,

sitting besides a Christall fountaine,

sitting besides a Christall fountaine, in shadow of a greene Oke   tree,

vppon his pipe this song playd   he: vntrue loue, vntrue loue, vn-

true loue, adew loue, adew loue, your minde is light,

FIG. 31.—Madrigal by William Byrde (1543–1623)
Seventeenth-Century Song, Fig. 63.   Eighteenth-Century Song, Figs. 110, 111

to listen to concerts on old instruments of this type on the wireless.

Another thing to be remembered is that we are in reality a very musical nation, with a great tradition of song behind us. During the last few years there has been a revival of singing in the villages, with musical festivals and competing choirs. People are rediscovering the joy of music. We have included in this edition a typical song for each century, and we are indebted for the choice to Mr. A. Forbes Milne. Fig. 31 gives the music and words of a madrigal by William Byrde (1543–1623). Here is a quotation from Thomas Morley's *Plaine and Easie Introduction to Practicale Musicke, set downe in the Form of a Dialogue* (1597). A party is described, and how "supper being ended, and musicke bookes (according to the custom) being brought to table, the mistresse of the house presented me with a part, earnestly requesting me to sing; but when, after many excuses, I protested unfainedly that I could not, every one began to wonder! Yes, some whispered to others, demanding how I was brought up; so that upon shame of mine ignorance, I goe now to seek out mine old friend Master Gnorimus to make myself his scholler."

Now let us make a big jump from musical to warlike exercises. Probably every village and township had butts, for shooting with the bow, and the name survives now in many places, like Newington Butts, in South London. The drawing shows that these must have been pleasant places to go to on a sunny afternoon, and watch the archers at practice.

Strutt thinks the cross-bow was introduced "not long before the commencement of the thirteenth century," but it suffered from this disadvantage that on a wet day the strings became useless; it could not be protected so easily as the long-bow, for which the archers had a canvas case, and it took longer to get ready for use. The cross-bow, like the early musket, seems to have been more used for sea fights and land sieges, where there was better cover, and less risk of the long-bowman turning the cross-bowman into an imitation of a feathered porcupine while he was getting ready.

In the regulations for use of the cross-bow we find, "In case any person should be wounded, or slain in these sports, with an arrow shot by one or other of the archers, he that shot the arrow was not to be sued or molested, if he had, immediately before the discharge of the weapon, cried out Fast! the signal usually given upon such occasions."

The Anglo-Saxons, Danes, and the Normans used the long-bow, and at Crécy and Agincourt it was the great weapon. Afterwards one hears that Henry v used gunpowder and guns, and the bow is forgotten, or thought of only as obsolete. This was not really so, and the first guns and muskets were cumbersome and feeble productions.

The long-bow lasted well on into the seventeenth century, and so late as Charles I commissions were appointed to survey land adjoining London, and restore it where the same had been encroached upon, so that the archers might practise. The best bows were made of yew, and in Edward IV's time the height of the bow was the same as that of the archer. The bowstring was of hemp, flax, or silk. The arrow used at Agincourt was a yard long. The steel or wand was made of ash, oak, or birch, and was feathered from the wing of a grey goose. The archer had a bracer, or close sleeve, laced on the left arm, so that the sleeve did not get in the way of the bowstring. A sixteenth-century writer gives instructions on how to stand when shooting, the way to hold the bow and draw the bowstring. A warning is given to watch the mark, not the arrow end. Certainly at this period, even though archery was beginning to be more of a sport than a warlike pursuit, the archers possessed far greater skill than we have any idea of; we are told of the archers "they would piece any armour."

From an old ballad about Robin Hood we gather that at a trial of archery before the king, "he clave the wand in two" from a distance of 400 yards. Cloudesle is made to give another proof of his skill, resembling that of William Tell. An apple is placed on his son's head at 120 yards distance.

> "And then drew out a fayre brode arrowe;
> Hys bow was great and longe,
> He set that arrowe in his bowe
> That was both styffe and stronge.
>
> Then Cloudesle cleft the apple in two,
> As many a man myght se;
> Over Gods forbode, sayde the kynge   (God forbid)
> That thou sholde shute at me."

An Act passed by Henry VIII ordered that no person who had reached the age of twenty-four years should shoot at any mark at less than 220 yards distance, so perhaps the 400 yards of Robin Hood was not an exaggeration. "Every village in time of war was expected to provide an archer, a gunman, a pike-man and a billman at the very least, as well as a store of corselets, almaines, rivets, shirts of mail and jacks quilted and covered with leather, fustian or canvas over thick plates of iron that are sewed in the same."

It is most interesting to watch the gradual development of the gun which was to supersede the bow. The gun developed from the cannon, and the earliest type of the latter was made from iron bars forged together and bound with hoops, the whole being mounted on a stout plank. Stone cannon balls were often used, hence the name some-times given, peterara. Gun-powder seems to have de-veloped from the Greek fire of mediæval times. The early gun was like a small cannon mounted on a stick, and fired by hand with a match, like the wick in a cigarette-lighter

FIG. 32.—Halberdier, 1572

of to-day. This type was used in the Wars of the Roses, and called a culverin.

The matchlock, arquebus, or serpentine was invented at the beginning of the sixteenth century, to do away with firing by hand. It continued in use until the seventeenth century, and the gunner used a rest which the man in Fig. 33 holds in his left hand. The early arquebusier could fire only ten to twelve shots in an hour, and at the end of Elizabeth's reign not more than thirty to forty. Wet weather spoiled the powder, wind and rain put out the match, and for a long time the bowmen laughed at it, and bow and musket were used side by side.

60

It is interesting to note that the first step towards our modern dragoons was taken by putting mounted arquebusiers in the battle of Pinkie, 1547, instead of using them as infantry. In the ballad of Brave Lord Willoughby, about 1588, we read:

" 'Stand to it, noble pikemen,
        And look you round about!
And shoot you right, you bowmen,
        And we will keep them out;

You musket and calliver men
        Do you prove true to me,
And I'll be foremost in the fight,'
        Says brave Lord Willoughby."

Henry VIII began to organise a regular army; each county was governed by a Lord Lieutenant, and it was his duty to appoint officers and procure a certain number of fighting men from each parish. All men belonging to the same band or levy were put into the uniform settled by their shire, and the only feature used in common was St. George's cross in red on the jerkin of each man.

FIG. 33.—Musketeer, 1550

Apart from the arming of individual soldiers, the cannon used towards the end of the century were far heavier and made more effective weapons than the primitive ordnance shown in illuminations of about 1500. Pl. 14, 1, shows graphically the storming of a city, with high walls, which have been considerably battered by the cannonade. It is interesting to see that the defenders reply with guns mounted in turrets. Pl. 14, 2, is from a careful contemporary drawing of the inside of a well-arranged siege battery, in active operation behind its protecting rampart of fascines.

61

Fig. 34.—The Assembly before the Hunt

(From *Du livre et de la Dresse*) *forestiation*

From archery and guns we can pass on to sport, and all boys and girls who are fond of hunting should read Turberville's *Booke of Hunting*, published in 1576, and reprinted by the Clarendon Press, 1908. It deals with "The Noble Arte of Venerie or Hunting—Wherein is handled and set out the Vertues, Nature, and Properties of siuetene sundrie Chaces together, with the order and maner how to Hunte and kill eueryone of them." So Turberville does for hunting at the end of the sixteenth century what Edward, Duke of York, did at the beginning of the fifteenth, and he, like the "Master of Game," must have been a delightful fellow, and his book is "great joy and liking" to the hunter of to-day. It deals with "houndes," and mentions fallow, "dunne, blacke houndes aunciently come from Sainct Hubert's Abbay in Ardene" as sixteenth-century breeds; the "best bringing up of whelpes" is discussed; "How a kennell ought to be situate and trimmed for Houndes," and their training is very carefully gone into.

Turberville devotes chapters to the "Nature and Subtilties of Hartes," and "How the Huntsman should go to seeke an Harte in small groues or hewts, beyng priuily enclosed within the greater springs in the Forests and strong couerts."

Our illustration, Fig. 34, is of a sixteenth-century meet, or "the place where and howe an assembly should be made, in the presence of a Prince, or some honorable person." Turberville breaks into rhyme about this, and says:

"The place should first be pight, on pleasant gladsome greene,
 Yet under shade of stately trees, where little sunne is seene;
 And neare some fountaine spring, whose chrystall running
      streames,
 May helpe to coole the parching heate, ycaught by Phœbus'
      beames."

Then we are told that "such a place once founde, the Butler first appeares," and he certainly does so to some purpose, because we are given details of the food provided for this substantial hunt breakfast, and Turberville goes off into verse again:

"For whiles colde kynes of Veale, colde capon, Beefe and Goose,
　With Pygeon pyes, and Mutton colde, are set on hunger loose,
　And make the forlorne hope, in doubt to scape full harde.
　Then come to giue a charge in flanke (else all the marte were
　　marde),
　First Neates' tongs poudred well, and Gambones of the Hogge,
　Then Saulsages and sauery knackes, to set men's myndes on
　　gogge."

We are not told if after all this they had a little nap, but meanwhile the harbouring of the deer and the setting of relays had been taking place. Turberville, in describing "How to set Relayes," says: "It is requisite to set men abroad which are brought up in hunting, and understande well their aduauntages, and with them a good pricker or huntsman on horsebacke, mounted upon a good curtall, which should be lightly clad, hauing good bootes and high, with an horne about his necke." At daybreak they have to get out for the place appointed for their relay, and leave their hounds coupled there at the foot of a tree. They then set out to see if they can "discouer the Hart"—this done, the huntsman must lead his hounds coupled or "tyed unto the tracke, and let them follow so three or foure paces right, then let him cast of one, and if he take it right, then may he uncouple the rest, and blowe to them."

"Then he which seemed to have harbored the greatest and oldest Deare reports to the Prince or Lord," who by this time has recovered from the hunt breakfast, and takes his "blood-hounde," with all the prickers or hunters on horseback, every one with a good cudgel in his hand "called a Hunting coodgell or a troncheon to turne the boughes and beare them from his face as he followeth the houndes in the woodes or thickes." The huntsman who has harboured the deer then goes "before them and rowze the deare, and then the rest cast off their houndes, and he and all of them crying, 'To him, to him! that's he, that's he!' and such other words of encouragement." The bloodhound was used at a check "untill they haue rowzed or founde him againe with their bloudhounde." Hounds were encouraged by name, thus, "Hyke a Bewmont, Hyke Hyke, to him, to him!" A great deal of interesting advice is given

PLATE 14

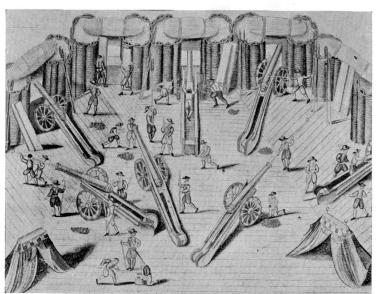

Contemporary Drawing

A Siege Battery in Active Operation

Contemporary Woodcut in Holinshed's "Chronicles"

Bombardment and Siege Attack of a Walled City

PLATE 15

Mid-Eighteenth-Century Engraving

Complete Design for Whitehall Palace, by John Webb and Inigo Jones

on how to overcome the many devices of the hart to escape pursuit. Chapter XLI deals with "Howe to kill an Hart when he is at bay, and what is then to be done." If the hart is in deep water the huntsman is to couple up his hounds, and "stand close and upon a cleare winde, he may chance to haue a blowe at him with his sworde as he (the hart) commeth out," or a boat is to be obtained, or if the huntsman can swim, he is to do so, dagger in hand, avoiding the "swrede blowe" the hart may give him.

"The breaking up of the Deare" is the incident chosen for our frontispiece, and is thus described. The Prince or chief alights "and takes essaye of the deare with a sharpe knyfe, the which is done in this manner. The deare being layd upon his back, the Prince, chiefe, or such as they shall appoint, commes to it: And the chiefe huntsman (kneeling, if it be to a Prince) doth holde the deare by the fore-foote, whiles the Prince or chief cut a slyt drawn alongst the brysket of the deare, somewhat lower than the brysket towards the belly. This is done to see the goodnesse of the flesh, and howe thick it is." Then "we use to cut off the deares' heades. And that is commonly done also by the chiefe personage." Various other portions of the hart are broken up and the hounds rewarded.

Here is a cap that fits as well to-day as it did in the sixteenth century:

"But noweadays I see fewe hunt the Harte as he ought to be hunted; for men give not their hounds leysure to hunt, neither is there passing two or three that can hunt: for there are so many hunters on horsebacke which can neither blow, hallow, nor prick perfectly, which mingle themselues amongst the hounds, crossing them, and breaking their course, in such sort, that it is not possible they should hunt truly: and therefore I say, that it is the horses which hunt, and not the hounds." So there were thrusters even in those days.

Turberville published as well *The Booke of Falconrie* in 1575, and we have given two of the illustrations from this in Figs. 35 and 36. He gives the details of hawking in the same way that he deals with hunting, and the drawings are excellent, with splendid details of the costume. The left-hand figure in Fig. 36 is wearing padded trunks which reach to the knees,

FIG. 35.—"To flye at the Hearon, according to Martine"

while his retainers still keep to the short trunks and trunk hose.

From sport in the country, we can pass to amusements in the towns, and here we must remember the great part played by the theatre in those times.

The old Morality Plays, to which we referred in Vol. I, still continued to be performed in the sixteenth century, but

66

FIG. 36.—From Turberville's *The Booke of Falconrie* (1575)

gradually, as the Renaissance opened up men's minds, and they became interested in classical literature, a new school of dramatists arose, until, at the end of the century, Shakespeare's genius was to make this period of the art for ever memorable. The publication of Spenser's *Faerie Queene*, about 1589, came as a revelation. The literary man of the early sixteenth century still thought of Latin as the only educated tongue, so that when the *Faerie Queene* was published it was not only the greatest poem since Chaucer's *Canterbury Tales*, but a vivid illustration of the possibilities of our language.

There were many dramatists before Shakespeare, doing spade work, but the first group which sprang into prominence was that which comprised Marlowe, Peele, Greene, and Nash. They worked between 1580 and 1590, and have been called the Bohemians; they introduced plays which were a picturesque jumble of good and bad, and a reflection of their own irregular lives. The sixteenth-century men and women can be accused of all the faults but dullness, and in their writing could take just the ordinary common words and set them down in such a way that the sentence sparkles and laughs at you, is sad and makes you want to cry.

Shakespeare started his theatrical life about 1585, and appears to have been able to gather up all the threads, and all the traditions, and weave them into his plays. Greene when dying is thought to have made complaint of this, and referred to his rival when he said: "An upstart crow beautified with our feathers—the only shakescene in the country." Chapman and Marston were companions of Shakespeare. Now, just as very little is known of Shakespeare himself, not a great deal is known of the Elizabethan theatre. Our drawing, Fig. 37, has been made from an original sketch of the Swan Theatre, by Johannes de Witt, who visited London about 1600. This was built at Bankside, in Southwark, on the south side of the Thames; then, as now, a rather grubby place. This, however, did not worry the sixteenth-century playgoer so much, because he went in a delightful way, by boat, the most usual method in those days of getting about London. There was also the "Rose" (1592), Shakespeare's "Globe," and the theatre in Shoreditch. Plays were often given in the galleried yards of inns, and we shall see later how this influenced the design of the theatres.

Another source of information on the Elizabethan theatre is a contract dated "the eighte daie of Januarye 1599," between "Phillipp Henslowe and Edwarde Allen—on th' one parte, and Peeter Streete, cittizein and carpenter—on th' other parte." Peeter agreed for £440 to build a "newe howse and stadge for a plaie-howse." Edward Alleyn, as the name is now spelled, founded Dulwich College in 1619, where the contract is preserved, and, like Shakespeare, appears to have made money, and led a sober life differing from the Bohemians. Henslow managed a company of players at the "Rose," of which Shakespeare was a member in 1592.

The theatre which Peeter built was called the "Fortune," and it was "scytuate and beinge nere Goldinge Lane in the parishe of Sainte Giles withoute Cripplegate." It was remark-

FIG. 37.—Elizabethan "Plaie" House

Seventeenth-Century Theatre, Fig. 77.   Eighteenth-Century Circus, Fig. 122

able in that it was square, and most of the others were circular. It was "to conteine fowerscore foote of lawfull assize everye waie square withoute, and fiftie-five foote of like assize square everye waie within." This gives us some idea of the size of the plan of the "Fortune." So far as height was concerned, the contract stipulated for "the said frame to conteine three stories in heighth, the first or lower storie to conteine twelve foote of lawfull assize in heighte, the seconde storie eleaven

69

foote, . . . and the third or upper storie . . . nyne foote. All which stories shall conteine twelve foote and a half of lawfull assize in breadth throughoute, besides a juttey forwardes in eyther of the saide twoe upper stories of tenne ynches of lawfull assize; with fower convenient divisions for gentlemen's roomes, and other sufficient and convenient divisions for twoepennie rooms." The "Fortune" was to be fitted up inside "with suche like steares, conveyances, and divisions, withoute and within, as are made and contryved in and to the late erected plaie-howse on the Banck, in the saide parishe

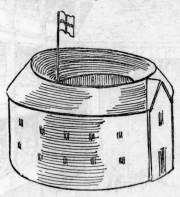

FIG. 38.—The "Globe"

of Saint Saviours, called the Globe; with a stadge and tyreinge-howse to be made, erected and sett up within the saide frame; with a shadowe or cover over the saide stadge." Later it is specified that "the same lower storie to be alsoe laide over and fenced with stronge yron pykes." Now, excepting only that the "Fortune" was square in plan, this contract very clearly agrees with the details of the "Swan" shown in Johannes de Witt's sketch, from which we have made our drawing. The "Globe" was octagonal in plan until is was burnt down in 1612, when it appears to have been rebuilt on circular lines like the "Swan." Our cut, Fig. 38, has been made from a print by Hollar of 1647 which shows this. Close by on the same print is another circular building called the "Beere baytine Hall" (Fig. 39), which shows how very similar the two sorts of buildings were. We know this was the case from Lambard's *Perambulation of Kent*, 1576, who says: "Those who go to Paris Garden (where the 'Swan' was), the 'Bell Savage' (an inn in Ludgate Hill), and the 'Theatre' (in Shoreditch) to behold bear-baiting, interludes, or fence play, must not account of any pleasant spectacle unless first they pay one penny at the gate, a second at the entry of the scaffold (or stage), and a third for quiet sitting." So that apparently the theatres were used for bear-baiting and wild beast shows if necessary. In the "Fortune" contract it is specified that the "lower storie be fenced off with strong yron pykes," which suggests that the wild beasts were to be kept safely in the pit. Both theatre and bear-baiting hall were built on much the same sort of plan, and undoubtedly founded on the ancient arenas where the spectators sat round and watched the spectacle, the galleries evidently being added after the fashion of the old inns like the "Bell Savage," to which people were accustomed.

Lambard tells us how you paid to go into the pit, and then more for the other parts of the house. The pit was open to the sky, and this, combined with the dangerous state of the streets after dark, and the difficulties of lighting, led to the performances being given in daylight. On a sunny day with a blue sky, and the gay colours of the people's dresses, the sight must have been a pretty one

FIG. 39.—"Beere baytine Hall"

indeed. The stage, as shown, was set up on a scaffold, and projected well into the yard or pit; it was open at the sides behind the columns, so that the people in the boxes there got a good view of what was going on. It is doubtful if the two doors at the back of the stage formed part of the structure, or were enclosed by a movable piece of scenery, behind which was an inner stage, which could be used to represent a cavern, or inner room, if needed by the play. The boxes over were undoubtedly called into use by the players, if a balcony or gallery became necessary. On the left-hand side of the stage are three gallants, and this was quite usual, and a position desired by the Elizabethan "blood."

The scenery is supposed to have been sketchy, and its

purpose was sometimes indicated by labels, so that there might be no mistake. Women did not act, and their parts were taken by boys. In the turret was a trumpeter, who tuned up when the play was about to begin. There is a moral in all this: if the Elizabethans were satisfied with an inn yard, or bear-baiting hall, as a quite sufficient background for their plays, then boys and girls of to-day might, with a little ingenuity and an equal enthusiasm, easily transform their ordinary school

FIG. 40.—Elizabethan Coach

Seventeenth-Century Vehicles, Fig. 67, Pl. 26.
Eighteenth-Century Vehicles, Figs. 115–119.

hall, courtyard, or corner of quad, into a theatre; a window can be found for Juliet. People hesitate to make the attempt, thinking they must have elaborate costume, whereas the play, with Shakespeare's wonderful language, and the interest of acting and action, is the thing if you are good enough at pretending.

Illustration No. 40 shows a state coach of the time of Elizabeth. This is interesting, because it marks a considerable development on the char shown in Vol. I (p. 166), and is evidence that people were beginning to want to travel about more. Coaches were so called because they were first made

at Kotze, in Hungary, in the fifteenth century. They were
introduced into England about 1555, and at first were very
simple in structure, and the occupants had to depend for
protection from the weather on curtains; but the seating is
that of the later-day coach, with seats in the boot at the sides.
The seventeenth century was the great time for the development in coach building, and we shall have more to say in the
next chapter. This drawing, however, is of value, because it
shows the early type, before there was any idea of suspending
the body by leather braces.

Although, with the introduction of printing, a wide field
of pleasure was opened to children, they did not reap the
real benefit of this great invention before the middle of the
seventeenth century. Printing was still so costly and books so
precious, that few if any, for children, are to be found before
that time. Nursery stories had always been told, handed down
from generation to generation by word of mouth, and lessons
were taught in the same way. Quite tiny children learned to
recite the Psalms in Latin, the Gloria in Excelsis, the Nicene
Creed, and the Paternoster, for, as there were so few books,
everything the children knew had to be learned by heart. At
the end of the fifteenth century the earliest form of school-
book, namely the horn-book, came into use. This was merely
an oblong piece of wood, shaped like a battledore, on which
was pasted a paper printed with the alphabet in black-letter,
or in Roman characters, the numerals, or the Ave and the
Paternoster. This was covered by a sheet of transparent horn,
and bound at the edge with brass. It had a wooden handle,
with a hole and string to hang it round the waist or neck. At
the beginning of the alphabet was a little cross, and on some
was written the rhyme:

> "Christe's cross be my speede
> In all vertue to proceede."

Because of this, children called it their criss-cross row.
Some of these horn-books had backs of embossed and gilded
leather. One can be seen held by a little girl of the seventeenth
century in Illustration No. 49. Since, however, this will hardly
be counted among children's amusements, let us return to

nursery tales and games. Nearly all our well-known fairy tales are very old indeed: "Beauty and the Beast" had its origin, it is thought, in a legend called the "Red Bull of Norroway," and is either Saxon or earlier. "Jack the Giant-Killer" and "Tom Thumb" are supposed to be legends from the days of King Arthur. Dolls are certainly equally old, and were bought largely at the big fairs which were held all over the country. St. Bartholomew's Fair was established in 1133. There were stalls of toys, sweets, and dolls, and until recent days dolls were often called "Bartholomew babies." The toys would be drums, hobby horses, popguns, and kites, and we read also of lambs, made of white wool spangled with gold, the head of composition and the cheeks painted red, with black spots for eyes. These lambs had horns and legs of tin and a piece of pink tape for the neckband. Trumpets were sold made of cows' horns, also hoops, and battledores and shuttlecocks, as well as pipes made from elder stems with the pith extracted. Boys could buy popguns with clay pellets to fire from them, and gilt gingerbread and peppermint drops at twenty a penny were known as early as the fourteenth century.

FIG. 41.—Embroidery

Thus we can see that children had plenty of choice in their toys, and we can imagine that their games, as well as those of their elders, were very varied. The game of bowls was popular; you will remember that Sir Francis Drake was playing at bowls when the Armada came in sight. Paume, a game played by the Normans, was still in existence and was the forerunner of our tennis of to-day. Here is a description of this game in 1591: "About 3 of the clocke ten of the Earle of Hertford's servants all Somersetshire men, in a square greene court, before her Majesty's windowe, did hang up lines, squaring out the forme of a tennis-court making a crosse line in the middle. In this square they (being stript out of their dublets) played five to five, with the hand-ball, at bord and cord (as they tearme it) to the great liking of her Highness." Many of the sports were very cruel, and bull-baiting, bear-baiting, and cock-fighting were favourites—and also tilting at the Quintain. Schoolboys were allowed once a year on Shrove Tuesday to bring their own cocks to their school to be matched against one another in the school cockpit.

Girls were taught won-derful stitches in their embroidery, and began when quite small with a sampler on which all the various stitches were practised. In the late six-teenth century several interesting books of pat-terns were published, the first time that we hear of anything of the kind. One title runs as follows: "Here foloweth certaine Patternes

FIG. 42.—Embroidery

of Cutworkes; newly invented and never published before. Also sundry sorts of spots, as flowers, birdes, and fishes, etc., and will fitly serve to be wrought, some with gould, some with silke, and some with crewell in coullers (colours); or otherwise at your pleasure. And never but once published before. Printed by Richard Shorleyker."

A kind of patterned lace worked with a needle was very popular at this date, and was called "point devisé." Another and entirely new amusement which came into being in the Elizabethan era was the creation and performance of masques. Tournaments had nearly disappeared, and though we read of "Triumphal Justs" at the Tiltyard as a feature of Elizabeth's Court, they were not nearly so frequent nor had they the same hold on the people as during the fifteenth century. Their place was taken by masques. The first we hear of these was in the reign of Henry VIII at his feast at Greenwich in 1513. The chronicle reads thus: "On the daie of the Epiphanie at night, the Kynge with xi. others wer disguised after the manner of Italie called a maske, a thing not seen afore in England; they wer appareled in garments long and brode wrought all with gold, with visers and cappes of gold."

Queen Elizabeth made many progresses through the country, and at each stopping-place she was welcomed with a pageant and masque generally embodying stories of the ancient gods and goddesses. At one place at which she stopped by a river side, the bushes were parted, and Father Neptune with attendant nymphs appeared and recited a long poem hailing her as Queen of the Seas; on another occasion a great pageant was awaiting her, with Venus in the middle, who also recited verses, handing over her sceptre of beauty to the Queen! An interesting account of a visit she made to a private house is told in a letter written by Sir Robert Sidney, younger brother of Sir Philip Sidney, in 1600. He says: "Her Highness hath done honour to my poor house by visiting me, and seemed much pleased at what we did to please her. My son made her a fair speech, to which she did give a most gracious reply. The women did dance before her, whilst the cornets did salute from the gallery; she did vouchsafe to eat two morsels of rich comfit cake, and drank a small cordial from a gold cup. She had a marvellous suit of velvet borne by four of her first women attendants in rich apparel; two ushers did go before, and at going upstairs she called for a staff, and was much wearied in walking about the house, and said she wished to

FIG. 43.—Countrywoman

come another day. Six drums and six trumpets waited in the court, and sounded at her approach and departure. My wife did bear herself in wondrous good liking, and was attired in a purple kyrtle, fringed with gold; and myself in rich band and collar of needlework, and did wear a goodly stuff of the bravest cut and fashion with an underbody of silver and loops. The Queen was much in commendation of our appearances, and smiled at the ladies, who in their dances often came up to the steps on which the seat was fixed, to make their obeysance, and so fell back into their order again. The younger Markham did several gallant feats on a horse before the gate, leaping down and kissing his sword, and then mounting swiftly on the saddle, and passed a lance with much skill. The day well-nigh spent, the Queen went and tasted a small beverage that was set out in divers rooms where she might pass;

FIG. 44.—Elizabethan Pages

and then in much order was attended to the Palace, the cornets and trumpets sounding through the streets. One knight (I dare not name) did say, the Queen had done me more honour than some that had served her better; but envious tongues have venomed shafts, and so I rest in peace with what has happened; and God speed us all, my worthy Knight."

At another pageant performed before Queen Elizabeth, there was a sham fight between two bands of men in two mock castles. This was in the Temple fields in Warwick. In this fight "mortyr-pieces, and calibers, and harquebuyces, fireworks, squibs, and balls of fire" were used. So realistic was the firing that a house in the village was set on fire and completely burned down. Fireworks had just come into use, and on another occasion we hear of a sham fort overthrown by a dragon "flieing and casting out huge flames and squibs and alighting on the fort set fyere therein." The Elizabethan era was a great period for feasts and merry-making; it was an intensely live time, and if men worked hard they played as well. Nearly all feast days had their own particular ceremony to be duly observed thereon. At Hok Tide, the men of

FIG. 45.—Sixteenth-Century Game, "Club Kayles"
Seventeenth-Century Game, Fig. 78. Eighteenth-Century Game, Fig. 123

Coventry took part in a tilting match representing, in dumb show, the defeat of the Danes by the English. On Corpus Christi Day, June 14th, miracle plays and stories from the Old Testament were performed in Coventry, on stages on wheels which were drawn about the city. The plays were written in rhyme. Of May Day and the morris dance more will be spoken later on, but an account here of a wedding may not come amiss. "First came the bridegroom with the young bachelors, each with bride lace upon branches of green broom tied to his left arm." "Then the bride, being attired in a gown of sheep's russet, and a kirtle of fine worsted, attired with abillement of gold, and her hair, as yellow as gold, hanging

78

down behind her, which was curious combed and plaited; she was led to church between two sweet boys, with bride laces and rosemary tied about their silken sleeves. There was fair bride-cup of silver gilt carried before her, wherein was a goodly branch of rosemary, gilded and very fair, hung about with silken ribands of all colours. Musicians came next, then a group of maidens, some bearing great bridecakes, others of garlands of wheat finely gilded; and thus they passed into the church." In Shakespeare's *Taming of the Shrew* is found the custom of all drinking in the church of the "bride-cup."

Illustration No. 45 shows a game popular from very early times. Now we call it "Ninepins," but then it went by the name of "Keyles" or "Kayles," and if as in the picture the pins were aimed at with a stick instead of a ball, it was called "Club Kayles." This game was often made the occasion for betting, and in some advice to apprentices written in the fifteenth century they are told to—

> "Exchewe allewey eville company,
> Kayles, carding, and haserdy."

The tailpiece shows a panel of sixteenth-century ornament, which like the architecture of the day was a mixture of old and new. The designers were fond of using some central feature like a lion's head, and taking from this straps, or bands, raised above a background with curling edges, the strap often piercing these, and finishing with pretty shaped ends. Another characteristic was the custom of cutting out a fretted pattern, and mounting on parts of it diamond and oval-shaped lozenges. This sort of ornament continued in James 1's reign.

FIG. 46.—Sixteenth-Century Ornament
Seventeenth-Century Ornament, p. 146. Eighteenth-Century Ornament, p. 215

CHAPTER II.—"Stuart" Period of Design, 1600–1699.

Dates	Kings and Queens of England and France.	Famous Men.	Great Events.	Principal Buildings.
1602		Cardinal Mazarin b.		Burton Agnes, Yorks, 1602–10
1603	James I., m. Anne of Denmark			Audley End, Essex, 1603–16
1604				
1605		Sir Thomas Browne b.—W.	Gunpowder Plot	Bramshill, Hants, 1605–12
1606		Rembrandt van Ryn b.—P.		Holland House
1607			Colonization of Virginia	
1608		John Milton b.—Pt.		
1609				
1610	Louis XIII. of France	Teniers the younger b.—P.		Wadham College, Oxford, 1610–
1611		John Webb b.—A.		Hatfield House
1612		Samuel Butler b.—W.		
1613				Bolsover Castle
1617			Voyage of Sir Walter Raleigh to Guiana	
1618		Richard Lovelace b.—Pt.	Voyage of the Mayflower	Aston Hall, Warwickshire, 1618–
		Sir Peter Lely b.—P.		
		Murillo b.—P.		
1619				Blickling Hall, Norfolk, 1619–20
1620		John Evelyn b.—W.		
1621		Andrew Marvell b.—Pt.	Impeachment of Bacon	
1622		Molière b.—W.		Banqueting Hall, Whitehall
1625	Charles I., m. Henrietta Maria of France		Expedition to Cadiz	
				St. Peter's, Rome, dedicated, 16
1626				Abbot's Hospital, Guildford
1627			War with France	
1628		John Bunyan b.—W.	Petition of Right	
1629			Dissolution of Third Parliament	Swakeleys House, Uxbridge
1630		Pieter de Hoogh b.—P.		S. M. della Salute, Venice
1631		John Dryden b.—Pt.		
1632		Samuel Pepys b.—W.		
		Christopher Wren b.—A.		
1633		Thomas Flatman (miniaturist) b.	Laud, Archbishop of Canterbury	Burford Priory Chapel
1634			First Levy of Ship-Money	
1635				Raynham House, Norfolk
1636				Oriel College, Oxford
1637		Meindert Hobbema b.—P.	Trial of Hampden	
1638			The Covenant	
1639				Clare College Bridge
1640		William Wycherley b.—W.		
1641			Impeachment and execution of Strafford	
1642		Sir Isaac Newton b.—W.	Attempted arrest of five members and Civil War	
1643	Louis XIV. of France		Siege of Gloucester	
1644		William Penn b.	Battle of Marston Moor	
1645			Battle of Naseby	
1646		Sir Godfrey Kneller b.—P.	King joins Scots at Newark	
1647			King is given up to Parliament. Escapes to Carisbrooke	
1648		Grinling Gibbons b.—S.	Second Civil War. Pride's Purge	Wilton House
1649	Oliver Cromwell		Trial and execution of the King	Ashburnham House
1650			Defeat of Montrose. Battle of Dunbar	
1651		Thomas Otway b.—Pt.	Charles II. invades England	
1652			War with Holland	
1653			The Protectorate	
1654				Thorpe Hall, Northants
1655			Treaty with France	Tyttenhanger, Herts
1656				
1657				
1658		Purcell b.—M.	Death of Cromwell. His son Protector	
1659			Quarrels between Parliament and Army	
1660	Charles II., m. Catherine of Braganza		Monk marches on London	
1661		Daniel Defoe b.—W.	Charles's First Parliament	
1664		Matthew Prior b.—Pt.		Versailles
1665			Great Plague	Ashdown House, Berkshire
1666		Sir John Vanbrugh b.—A.	Fire of London	Brasenose College Chapel
1667		Swift b.—W.	Dutch on the Thames, and the Peace of Breda	Trinity College Chapel, Oxfor
1668			The Triple Alliance	
1669				
1670		Congreve b.—W.	Treaty of Dover	St. Katherine College, Cambrid 1670–80
1671		Colley Cibber b.—W.		
1672		Addison b.—W.	Second Dutch War	St. Stephen's, Walbrook, 1672–
1673			Test Act. Fall of the Cabal	Brewers' Hall
1674		Isaac Watts b.—Hymn W.		Middle Temple, 1674–84
1675				St. Paul's Cathedral begun
1676		Richard Steele b.—W.		
1677			Marriage of William of Orange and Princess Mary	
1678		Lord Bolingbroke b.	The Popish Plot	Trinity College Library, C bridge
1679		Thomas Parnell b.—Pt.	Habeas Corpus Act	
1680				Invalides, Paris
1681				
1682				Chelsea Hospital
1683			The Rye House Plot	Town Hall, Guildford
1684				Hall, Winchester College
1685	James II., dep. 1688; m. (1) Anne Hyde; (2) Mary of Modena	John Sebastian Bach b.—M	Insurrection of Monmouth. Battle of Sedgemoor	
		Handel b.—M.		
1687			Declaration of Indulgence	
1688		Alexander Pope b.—Pt	Invitation to William of Orange	Bluecoat School, Westminster
1689	William III., m. Mary of England	Richardson b.—W.		Hampton Court, 1689–1700
1694		Earl of Chesterfield b		
1695				Greenwich Hospital
1696				
1697		William Hogarth b.—P.		
1699		Joseph Chardin b.—P.		

A. = Architect.   P. = Painter.   Pt. = Poet.   S. = Sculptor.   W. = Writer.   M. = Musician.

16th-Century Chart, p. xvi.   18th-Century Chart, p. 148.

FIG. 47.—Horseman, time of Charles II
Horseman, Tudor, Fig. 2.　　　Horseman, Georgian, Fig. 80

CHAPTER II

THE SEVENTEENTH CENTURY

IT cannot be said that the Stuart period fulfilled the pro-
mise of the end of the sixteenth century. When Elizabeth
died, conditions seemed to point to a peaceful and happy
time; yet in a few years the seeds of civil war had been sown.
The Tudors had done their job magnificently, and when their
line came to an end England stood well with the world; no
Dutchman burned our ships in the Medway, and we had
produced a race of men whose names still make the blood
tingle. It was because of all this that Englishmen put up with
an absolute rule, for the Tudors not only ruled, but served
their people as well.

When James I came to the throne in 1603 he suffered from the disadvantage that he was not an Englishman. We talk now of a Briton, and the Scots, Irish, Welsh, and English pull together and think of Great Britain as their country, but not so the men of the seventeenth century, with ages of strife behind them; to them James was a poor man coming into a rich inheritance, and a foreigner as well. So he could not emulate the intimate rule of the Tudors and was kept somewhat at arm's length; also the fact that his mother, Mary Queen of Scots, had met her death in England, did not in all probability endear Englishmen to him.

It was in reality want of tact, as much as anything else, that brought Charles I into the collision with his Parliament which resulted in his tragic death. As well, there was the failure to realise that a people so much alive and interested in things as the seventeenth-century men, would insist on their share in the government of their country. The collision was inevitable; Cromwell was bound to win through, and to him must be given the credit for again winning for England that respect abroad which the Stuarts had thrown away.

The seventeenth century we know was a troublesome one and full of unrest and internal war, and yet reading through lives of families of the period, we gain the impression that except for the parts in which was actual conflict and allowing for the poverty and difficulties caused by the strife, life jogged on in the country districts pretty much as hitherto.

We read many accounts of gardens of flowers, fruit and vegetables, and Mr. Isham writes to Lady Verney that he will do up and send her sugar for preserving "if she hath currants e'now for this last wick of winds hath been so big that most of them are blowed off the trees." We read also of stew ponds of fish to be cleaned out and requests to the farmer to set the decoy for the wild fowl. Households did not change much; gentlewomen, if unmarried, became "helps and gentlewomen" to their relations, for the ladies of the house were still expected to superintend and if necessary take part in all the labours of the household. In Gervase Markham's *English Housewife*, published 1631, the title page reads: "The English housewife, containing the inward and outwards vertues which ought to be in a compleat woman. As her skill in Physick, Chirurgery, Cookery, extraction of oils, banquetting stuff, ordering of great feasts, preserving of all sorts of wines, conceited secrets, distillations of perfumes, ordering of wool, hemp or flax, making cloth and dying, the knowledge of dairies, the office of malting, of oats, their excellent uses in families, of brewing, baking and all other things belonging to a household." When one reads this formidable list one realises that the mistress would have great need of her unmarried relations to help her. Large households were still more or less self-supporting, cooking was on the same generous scale as in the sixteenth century.

The cultivation of sugar in the West Indies augmented its importation in England, and it began to take the place of the earlier honey. Rum was another discovery and was largely used by the Navy. A writer says: "Sugar canes distilled a hot hellish and terrible liquor called rum." Gin was also made, so called because it was flavoured with juniper. One great advantage to the country housewife was the institution of the carrier's cart, which ran through many districts twice a week, and from

FIG. 48.—Officer, Fifth Foot, 1688

many large places, Tonbridge for one, the post (by coach) went to London each day. Roads were still bad; lawlessness was still rife. An effort was made to cope with the hordes of beggars by issuing, each parish, to sundry poor persons unable to earn their living, badges giving them licence to beg, those begging without these badges to be imprisoned and otherwise punished. Those tramping the country to sell their goods were also given hawkers' licences as an assurance of their genuineness. Yet despite this, in the time of Charles I a kind of market grew up at the entrance to the palace precincts which was the scene of such confusion, noise and squalor, that a rule limiting it was made and orders given for officers to ride through the mob of hucksters and retainers and arrest all disorderly persons.

Nevertheless legitimate trade was fast increasing; the East India Company was founded in 1600 and it was a recognised thing that younger sons were sent abroad to learn about and start some trade. One of the Verney sons went to France and another to Spain for the purpose of learning the leather trade. The Vauxhall glass works were opened in 1670, when workmen brought from Venice blew glass and made mirrors.

Now we can find out what the seventeenth-century men and women looked like. During the reign of James 1, bombasted breeches and the monstrous farthingale were still worn, but with Charles 1 came a sudden reaction. The first man in the illustration (Pl. 16) belongs to this period. He is a Cavalier. His dress is rich, but simpler than that of the Elizabethan period. His hair is long, and the ruff has given place to a large lace-edged collar and cuffs. His coat fits loosely to the figure, and is braided and tagged round the waist. These tags were silken laces fastened to the breeches beneath, and drawn through eyelet holes in the tunic and knotted above; they answered the purpose of braces; stockings were also fastened to breeches in the same way. Sleeves were cut to show the shirt beneath, and a wide cloak was worn. Breeches were still full, but no longer padded, and two pairs of stockings were often worn—the outer pair shorter than the inner, and edged with lace, which showed above the top of the wide boot.

Ear-rings were fancied by the young beaux, who even painted their faces. The following is an interesting account of a little boy's clothes. His age was eight. He wore for winter a baize gown faced with fur; for high days his suit was of ash-coloured satin, doublet hose, stockings with silk garters and roses all to match, with an embroidered girdle and a cloak of the same colour, trimmed with squirrel fur. He had also a taffeta pickadel and ruff, and his sword fastened with a green scarf. He wore out five pairs of shoes in the year.

Ladies' skirts, although full, were no longer stretched out on a frame, but were caught back to show an embroidered petticoat underneath. Satin and stiff silk, or velvet, were largely used for the dresses, which were cut low on the shoulder, and

PLATE 16

Costume.   Seventeenth Century

Sixteenth-Century Costume, Pl. 4.   Eighteenth-Century Costume, Pl. 35, 36, and 37

finished with a delicate muslin and lace collar, with cuffs to match. Long gauntlet gloves were largely worn, and fashionable ladies sometimes wore as many as three pairs, one on top of the other, each pair very beautifully embroidered. The hair was drawn off the face into a knot behind, and the side pieces fell in ringlets on to the shoulders. Masks were always worn by the Court ladies in public; it was considered immodest to appear without one. From this has come the term "barefaced."

Our second man is a Puritan—one of those who, protesting against the follies of the fashionable world, wore always the opposite of the prevailing mode. See his plain hat without a feather, his closely cropped hair, and his clothes of sombre hue. Notice, too, his collar and cuffs without lace, and the lack of any trimming on his coat and breeches. From this cropped head sprang the term "Roundhead," distinguishing the Puritans from the Cavaliers in the Civil War of 1640. His lady's dress is very simple too; dull in colour, lacking all trimmings, with plain collar and cuffs, and a large white apron. Fashionable women also wore occasionally small aprons of delicate silk and lace, though of course neither so large nor plain as that of a Puritan. During the Commonwealth the more sober method of dress was general, but with Charles II came a renewal of fine clothes and bright colours, and in the reaction from the dull garments of the time gone by, folks were very gay indeed. The last couple belong to this time. The lady's hair is arranged in masses of ringlets, but occasionally on elderly women were seen wigs, much curled, and standing up high above the forehead.

Bodices were now peaked, and the full sleeves were open in front and caught together with jewelled clasps. Skirts were wide and dresses were made of beautiful materials, either satins or rich silks.

The lady wears a wide cloak held with a jewel on one shoulder, and out of doors she would have a large hooded cloak, or sometimes a hood alone. Pepys says in 1665: "To church, it being Whit Sunday, my wife, very fine in a new yellow bird's-eye hood as the fashion is now." Masks have gone out of fashion.

John Evelyn in 1664 writes: "I now observed that women

began to paint themselves, formerly a most ignominious thing."

Again, in his diary of 1666, he gives us some idea of ladies' dress of a more sporting character. He says: "The Queen was now in her Cavalier riding habit, hat and feathers and horseman's coat, going to take the air." Pepys gives us a more detailed account: "Walking in the galleries at Whitehall I find the Ladies of Honour dressed in their riding garbs with coats and doublets with deep skirts just for all the world like mine, and buttoned in their doublets up to the breast, with periwiggs and with hats, so that only for a long petticoat dragging under their men's coats, nobody could take them for women in any point whatever, which was an odd sight."

FIG. 49.—A Little Schoolgirl (1667) holding her Horn-book

On the third man we can see that the tunic of Charles I's reign has given place to that which is the beginning of the coat and waistcoat, and that sleeves are no longer slit, but are turned back at three-quarter length with wide cuffs, showing his full shirt sleeves, edged at the wrist with a frill. Wide collars had gone out of fashion and were replaced by a small lace cravat; men carried muffs in the street, and we read in Pepys' diary that he took his wife's muff for his own use and bought her a new one—just the sort of thing the old villain would do. Breeches were edged with a deep lace frill and were rosetted at the knee; they were of the same colour as the coat. Stockings and shoes took the place of high boots, and the shoes were long, narrow, buckled, and very square in the toe. Wigs, long and much curled, were seen on every man. It is said that they came into fashion with the Restoration, for many men with the cropped head of the Commonwealth desired to conceal their former principles and to imitate as nearly as possible the Cavalier love-locks; so they wore wigs.

Little boys wore long coats nearly reaching to their ankles for ordinary wear, but when they were put into coat and waistcoat they were often made to wear corsets to make their long straight waist-coats set well.

A charming letter written in the late seventeenth century and found in the *Lives of the Norths* gives an account of the breeching of a little boy Frank, of six years old. "You cannot beleeve the great concerne that was in the whole family here, last Wednesday, it being the day that the taylor was to helpe to dress little Frank in his breeches, in order to the making

FIG. 50.—Small Boy of 1633

an everyday suit by it. Never had any bride that was to be drest upon her wedding night more hands about her, some the legs and some the arms, the taylor butt'ning, and others putting on the sword, and so many lookers on, that, had I not a ffinger amongst them I could not have seen him. . . . They are very fitt, everything, and he looks taller and prettyer than in his coats (petticoats). Little Charles reyoiced as much as he did, for he jumpt all the while about him, and took notice of everything. I went to Bury and bo't everything for another suitt which will be finisht upon Saturday. So the coats are to be quite left of on Sunday. . . . When he was drest he asked Buckle whether muffs were out of fashion because they had not sent him one."

Fig. 50 shows the dress of a small boy of 1633, before he was breeched. His tunic and skirt are of scarlet trimmed with gold, and he has a white lawn collar and cuffs, and undersleeves of the same material which shows inside the open outer sleeve.

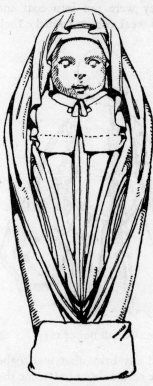

FIG. 51.—Baby in Swaddling Clothes, Ickenham, Middlesex (1665)

Fig. 51 shows a baby in swaddling clothes taken from a tomb, dated 1665, in Ickenham church. Fig. 52 is the portrait of a widow, dated 1632.

Mourning was made the occasion of great ceremony and the rules regarding mourning were rigid. Black bed-hangings were considered necessary and in the Verney family in 1650 was a great black bed that went the rounds of the family as deaths occurred. Mourning was sent also to intimate friends as well as to relations. A black coach, that is, a coach covered with a black cloth, was used, the servants' saddles also being covered in black.

Having gained some idea of the appearance of the people, we can now turn to the Navy, and here we shall find notable developments in shipbuilding; but if the ships were better, the sailormen, with a few exceptions, do not compare favourably with those of the sixteenth century. We know a great deal of their doings because of a diary to which we have already referred, written by Pepys, between 1660 and 1669, when he was a clerk in the Navy Office. Later on, in 1673, he was made Secretary of the Navy, when James II, then Duke of York, was Lord High Admiral. James was a good friend to the sailors, and was very ably helped by Pepys. His diary is of the greatest interest because it deals with all sorts of things besides Navy affairs, and is of the greatest importance for the sidelights so thrown upon history. The diary was written in a shorthand invented by Pepys, and evidently gave him a great deal of pleasure; here he put down all sorts of notes, not thinking they would ever be discovered, and so to-day we can really know what were the thoughts of a notable man in the seventeenth century. Curious that a book, written in such fashion, should be one of the most famous in the English language.

FIG. 52.—A Widow of 1632

To go back to the beginning of the century. James I was too mean to spend money on the Navy, and was content with the laurels gained in Elizabeth's time. Charles I was more conscientious, and encouraged shipbuilding. It was during his reign (1637) that the *Sovereign of the Seas* was designed by Phineas, and built by Peter Pett, and we have selected this boat for our illustration, Fig. 53. Her length was 169 feet 9 inches, beam 48 feet 4 inches, and depth of hold 19 feet 4 inches, tonnage 1683. Remember that, before 1628, tonnage was reckoned by the space sufficient to stow a tun of wine = 42 cubic feet. After that date, it was length of keel × greatest breadth of beam × depth ÷ 100. The Pett family were naval architects and boat builders from the time of Henry VIII to William and Mary, and we hear about them from Pepys. The *Sovereign* was considered a very wonderful boat, and saw service under Blake. She was the first boat to carry royals and top-gallants on all masts. The cut of the sails should be noticed, and how they belly out much more than was the case later on. One lateen remains on the mizzen, but

FIG. 53.—The *Sovereign of the Seas*

Mediterranean Galley, Fig. 9.   Galleon, Fig. 10.   *Ark Royal*, Fig. 11.
Eighteenth-Century Ship, Fig. 85.   Clipper, Fig. 86

over this we now have square sails. There is a spritsail under
the bowsprit, and an amusing square sail on the sprit topmast
over it. It should be noticed that the lines of the hull still
show a likeness to the galley: there is the same snaky build,
with beak head and high poop. John Evelyn, the other great
seventeenth-century diarist, writing of the *Sovereign*, says she
was called the *Golden Devil* by the Dutch, from the amount of
carving and gilding on her stern. She was remodelled in 1684
and called the *Royal Sovereign*, and finally was burnt at Chatham
in 1696.

Charles at his death left the Navy weak, though as an instrument in Cromwell's hands it was used to enforce respect for
us abroad. The Dutch War of 1652–54 produced our great
admiral, Robert Blake, who fought against Tromp and De
Ruyter. The next Dutch War of 1665–67 found us very
unprepared, as Pepys said: "For we do nothing in this office

like people able to carry on a war." The Great Plague of 1665 of course handicapped our effort, but bribery and corruption was the order of the day and did far more harm than the Plague. Even Pepys, who was an honest man for the time, had his price, but excuses himself, when taking a present, by not looking at it, "that I might say that I did not know what there was in the bag." The Dutch sailed up to Chatham in 1667, and burned our ships there.

This was rather sad, for only a few years before they had given us the subject of our illustration, Pl. 17. This has another interest, because it shows the first vessel to which the name of "yacht" was given in England. Evelyn wrote in his diary, for October 1, 1661: "I sailed this morning with his Majesty in one of his yachts (or pleasure boats), vessels not known among us till the Dutch East India Company presented that curious piece to the King." The "curious piece" arrived in England in this fashion. When Charles II was recalled to England, he sailed to meet the English fleet in a Dutch yacht, escorted by twelve others. Charles remarked on the handiness of the little vessels which had been evolved on the water-ways of Holland. The Dutchmen, realising that Charles, as King of England, would be a much more influential person than the exile they had known since 1649, asked him to accept a yacht which was then building, and which was sent to England subsequently. Charles acknowledged its receipt, writing in French, thus: "Maintenant vous avez encore rafraichie Nostre memoire par un nouveau present d'un Yaugh, des plus jolys et des plus agreables a nostre humeur qu'on auroit pu inventer." This letter was dated August 16, 1660. Pepys went to see the Dutch boat with Pett, the shipbuilder, on November 8, 1660, and noted that he was to build an English one to outdo it.

By January 13, 1661, Pett's yacht was so far advanced that Pepys could see it, and report that it was "a pretty thing, and much beyond the Dutchman's." Later we read of the yachts racing from Greenwich to Gravesend and back, attended by barges and kitchen boats. The Dutch boat was called *Mary*, and our illustration, Pl. 17, has been made from a drawing of the hull by W. Van de Velde, Jun., in the British Museum.

and another by J. Storck, which shows its rigging. The subject is fully treated in the *Mariner's Mirror* for October 1919, Vol. v., No. IV. Mr. Sopwith's challenger for the America's cup, *Endeavour*, and the defender *Ranger* are lineal descendants of the *Mary*.

Pls. 18 and 19, from *Mr. Dummer's Draughts of the Body of an English Man-of-War*, about 1680, are interesting seventeenth-century parallels to the illustrations with which we are familiar to-day showing the insides of steamships. These are not, as a rule, works of art, whereas there can be no doubt that Mr. Dummer was a fine draughtsman.

FIG. 54.—Schoolmaster, 1631

The last Dutch War of the seventeenth century was between 1671–74, and the honours seem to have been pretty evenly divided with our sturdy foes. The most memorable result was that we gained New Amsterdam, and renamed it New York, after James, Duke of York, who was later on to be James II. The rivalry ceased with the accession of William and Mary. Evelyn has a note in his diary in 1683, which shows how bad things were at the end of Charles II's reign. "This summer did we suffer twenty French men-of-war to pass our Channel towards the Sound, to help the Danes against the Swedes, who had abandoned the French interest; we not having ready sufficient to guard our coasts or take cognizance of what they did; though the nation never had more, or a better navy, yet the sea had never so slender a fleet."

The diary of Henry Teonge is very interesting for the light it throws on life inboard. Teonge was a Navy chaplain between

1675–79, and must have been a sporting parson, because he was fifty-four when he first went to sea; yet he declared, "no life at the shoare being comparable to this at sea, where we have good meate and good drinke provided for us, and good company, and good divertisments; without the least care, sorrow or trouble," which sounds as if times had been hard for him before. His first trip was in the *Assistance*. They started from the Thames, and at Dover the captain's wife, and other ladies, were put ashore "with 3 cheares, 7 guns, and our trumpets sounding." This practice led to a regulation: "And, forasmuch as the Harbouring of Women and Children on board his Ma^{ts} Shipps in Ordinary may expose them to accidents . . . as well as Inconveniences of other kinds, We doe hereby strictly forbid the Lodgeing or keeping of any Women or Children on board the sd. Shipps on any pretence whatsoever." Teonge's description of the food is quite appetising. Off Lisbon "our noble Capt. feasted the officers of his small squadron with 4 dishes of meate, viz., 4 excellent henns and a peice of pork boyled, in a dish; a giggett of excellent mutton and turnips; a peice of beife of 8 ribbs, well seasoned and roasted; and a couple of very fatt greene geese; last of all a greate chesshyre cheese." As they drank "Canary, Sherry, Renish, Clarett, white wine, syder, ale, beare and punch" one understands why the Captain is called noble.

The men's food was bread or biscuit, beer, beef, pork, peas, oatmeal, flour, and suet, butter, and cheese.

At Gibraltar, "every on that hath not yet beene in the Straites pays his dollar, or must be duckt at yard arme." Discipline was maintained; on Monday mornings boys who had misbehaved during the week past were "whipt with a catt with 9 tayles for their misdemeanurs, by the boarson's mate." Again, two men and a boy had "an iron pinn clapt closse into their mouths, and tyd behind their heads; and there they stood a whole houre . . . an excellent cure for swearers"—but a rather rough one.

The *Assistance* helped at the blockade of Tripoli, and the boatswain died. "He had a neate coffin, which was covered over with on of the King's jacks, and his boarson's sylver

93

whisle and chaine layd on the top betweene 2 pistolls crost
with a hangar drawne. At his going off the ship he had 9 gunns,
which were fyred at a minut's distance. And 8 trompetts
sownding dolefully, whereof the 4 in the first ranke began
and the next 4 answered, so that ther was a continued dolefull
tone from the ship to the shoare, and from thence to the grave.

FIG. 55.—Sweep, 1688

Halfe the ship's company,
with their musketts in the
right posture, going after
the corps, with all the officers
of all the ships that were
there. . . . When he was
buryed he had 4 peales of
muskett shott. And as soone
as we were out of the church
yard the trumpetts sounded
merry levitts all the way."
On Christmas Day aboard
ship the trumpeters tuned up
outside the cabin doors,
"playing a levite at each
cabine doore, and bidding
good morrow, wishing a
merry Christmas"; for
dinner they "had excellent
good fayre; a ribb of beife,
plumb puddings, minct
pyes." On Twelfth Night
"wee had a greate kake
made, in which was put a
beane for the King, a pease for the Queen, a cloave for the
knave, a ragg for the slutt. The kake was cutt into severall
peices in the great cabin, and all putt into a napkin, out of
which every on took his peice as out of a lottery: then each
peice is broaken to see what was in it, which caused much
laughter." Nice old sailormen.

Herrick, the seventeenth-century poet, who was born in
1591 and died 1674, wrote a poem on "Twelfe Night, or
King and Queene." Here are two verses:

"Now, now the mirth comes
    With the cake full of plums,
Where Beane's the King of the
        sport here,
    Beside we must know,
    The Pea also
Must revell, as Queene, in the
        Court here.

"Begin then to chuse,
    (This night as ye use)
Who shall for the present de-
        light here,
    Be a King by the lot,
    And who shall not
Be Twelfe-day Queene for the
        night here."

Reverting to sailormen, it was in the reign of William and Mary that Greenwich Hospital was founded as a home for old seamen, and was built from the design of Sir Christopher Wren. John Evelyn was the first Treasurer. Attention began to be paid to lighting the coasts, and the first Eddystone Lighthouse was built 1694–98, but was destroyed by a great storm in 1703. The illustration, Pl. 20, shows that it was a queer fantastic structure, recalling a Chinese pagoda. Its design and erection were due to a curious character, Henry Winstanley, engraver and engineer, of Essex; his charming little house at Littlebury, near Saffron Walden, is shown in Fig. 56. He engraved a whole set of plates of the great house of Audley End, in Essex, which is very valuable as showing a great court which has since utterly vanished. He also engraved a fine Tudor house at Rycote, Oxfordshire, which has all but entirely disappeared. When working on the lighthouse he was carried off by a French privateer and the work destroyed, but he was exchanged and finished it. He always said he wished for nothing better than to be in it during a great storm, and his wish was fulfilled, in the great tempest of November 27, 1703; when it had passed, nothing was left of this Heath Robinson erection or of its designer and his five companions. The versatile Winstanley had also specialised in ingenious hydraulic devices, fantastic but quite useless, of which he made shows at the Water Theatre in Piccadilly. His widow continued to show them there and at his house as late as 1714. There were water-playing mermaids, gods and goddesses, a fiery dragon belching forth fireballs, and a "Curious Barrel" which spouted all sorts of pleasant drinks and served in turn in a Spring Garden and a Dairy House.

Leaving the sea and going ashore, the illustration, Pl. 22,

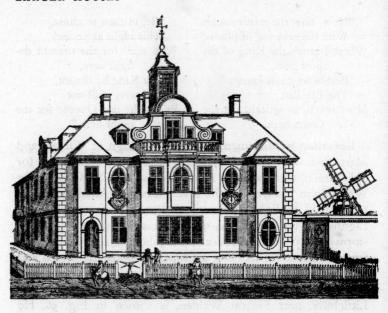

FIG. 56.—Winstanley's House at Littlebury, Essex
No longer existing

shows a house of the middle of Charles I's reign. That monarch was a great patron of the arts, and one of the first to start collections of pictures; with his French wife he probably led the way, and helped to make fashionable the new Renaissance style of architecture, of which we saw the beginnings in the last century. This particular house is interesting because, so far as its exterior is concerned, it does not jump a long way ahead of such houses as Blickling and Hatfield, built in James I's reign. It is still gabled, though the gables have as terminations the classical feature called a pediment; the general outline then follows on traditional lines, though the detail is more scholarly than before. The windows were originally glazed with leaded lights in the form of casements, hinged at the sides like doors, not as sashes sliding up and down, but were grouped in a different way from those of the sixteenth century. This example was converted to the sash type of window when altered by William Kent about 1730.

The first Eaton Hall, Chester, seen in Pl. 29 and erected

PLATE 17

Charles II "Yaugh"

The Stern of the *Royal Charles*,
a First Rate, built in 1673

The Stern of an English Second
Rate of the smaller class, 1670

From Drawings by Van de Velde

PLATE 18

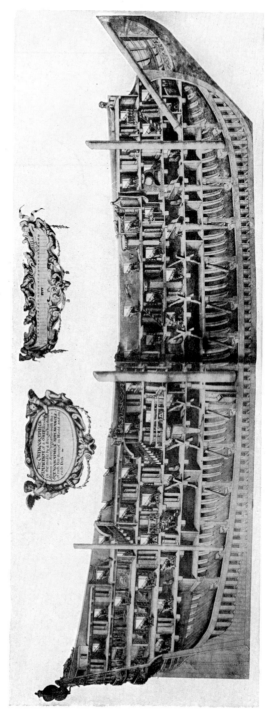

Combined Photograph of Dummer's Longitudinal Section of a First-Rate

PLATE 19

Stern of H.M.S. *London*. From a Drawing by Van de Velde, Jun.

PLATE 20

Engraving by the Designer

The first Eddystone Lighthouse, designed by Henry Winstanley.
Destroyed by Storm, 1703

PLATE 21

The Saloon, Raynham Hall, Norfolk, 1636

Probably designed by the Owner, Sir Roger Townshend, altered by William Kent, c. 1730

Jacobean Interiors, Fig. 26, Pls. 10, 27. Eighteenth-Century Interiors, Figs. 99, 111, Pl. 38

PLATE 22

Raynham Hall, Norfolk 1636

Probably by Sir Roger Townshend, altered to Sash Windows by William Kent, c. 1730

Timber-framed House, Fig. 15. Sixteenth-Century Stone House, Pls. 8, 9. Eighteenth-Century Houses, Pl. 29, Fig. 96.
Eighteenth-Century Town House, Fig. 97

The Interior

The Tower

Willen Church, Buckinghamshire

PARISH CHURCH
OF ST. MARY
MAGDALENE
WILLEN
BUCKS

PLATE 24

The Courtyard
The Almshouses at Amersham, Buckinghamshire
Built by Sir Wm. Drake, 1657

about the end of the century shows a further development towards the classic style. It is a pleasing, restrained design with two large kitchen and stable blocks set at right angles.

When we get to the inside of the house, Pl. 21, we find that, though the exterior has points of resemblance with Blickling and Hatfield, the interior has in reality jumped far ahead of these houses; so much is this the case that for perhaps the only time in our book the architecture and dress of the period do not go together—the latter has an old-fashioned look. It may be that the owner, Sir Roger Townshend, who was largely his own architect, wished the outside of his house to be homely, but did not mind the interior being fashionable; actually most of the inside had to be finished later on.

Inigo Jones, who did work of this character, was born in 1573 and died 1652, and must be reckoned as the first English architect of consequence. Thorpe, who lived in the reigns of Elizabeth and James, was working as early as 1570, and Smithson, who died in 1634, have left collections of drawings of houses, but they must be thought of as belonging to the old school of building by a group of men associated together, each designing his own part of a traditional treatment, for which Thorpe, or Smithson, may have supplied the general lay-out. Jones, and his kinsman and pupil Webb, and the later architects, designed the whole, and their work was very good and scholarly, if somewhat lacking in the interest of the earlier method. Talking of his early training, Inigo Jones said: "Being naturally inclined in my younger years to study the arts of design, I passed into foreign parts to converse with the great masters thereof in Italy, where I applied myself to search out the Ruins of those ancient Buildings, which, in despite of Time itself and violence of Barbarians, are yet remaining. Having satisfied myself in these, and returning to my native country, I applied my mind more particularly to the study of Architecture." A second visit was paid in 1613–14, so Inigo Jones was well equipped; he designed the Banqueting Hall in Whitehall for James I, and this was finished in 1622. Boys and girls who know this building should study it, and realise that it is fully classical in style and modelled on the "Ruins of those ancient Buildings" which Jones saw in Italy, and that it was the first of its kind in England. As such it is an astonishing production, and the fruit of a great mental effort —but Inigo was a genius, and to such all things are possible.

But the Banqueting Hall is only a small fragment of the vast scheme for the Palace of Whitehall, a design of stupendous magnificence prepared largely by Inigo Jones' nephew, John Webb. Many drawings of it exist, but this illustration (Pl. 15) is from a very large bird's-eye reconstruction prepared about the middle of the eighteenth century.

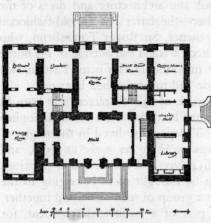

FIG. 57.—Plan of Raynham Hall, shown in Pls. 21–22.

The Saloon of Raynham Hall, Pl. 22, is a restrained classic design, remarkable for its deeply recessed ceiling modelled in high relief, with painted panels. This is probably largely as originally built, though the cornice, chimneypiece, and ceiling paintings are due to William Kent, who is responsible for practically all the other interiors in the house; they are good designs in the Palladian style, dating just about a hundred years after the house was actually erected. Jones did a very beautiful double cube room at Wilton about 1649, and was very successful with his interiors.

The plan of the house, Fig. 57, again marks a definite change. The hall now becomes a place of entrance only, and the whole arrangement is more modern in treatment. The kitchen and servants have been banished to the basement, and master and man no longer meet on common ground.

Sir Christopher Wren was a worthy successor to Jones and Webb; born in 1632, he first attracted attention as an astronomer and mathematician, and turned to architecture later on. Wren carried out the Sheldonian Theatre at Oxford between 1663–68. In the latter year he was appointed Surveyor to His Majesty's

Works. Webb had hoped to obtain the appointment, but was not in favour through work done during the Commonwealth. All boys and girls know that Wren designed St. Paul's Cathedral, and many of the City churches, some of which the English pulled down and the Germans have bombed.

In addition to London, there are groups of Renaissance churches at Bristol, badly bombed, and Worcester. Though not very common, there are quite a number of Renaissance country churches scattered about, especially in the Midlands, and for the first time Mr. Marcus Whiffen has told us about them in *Stuart and Georgian Churches*—1603–1837, issued in 1948. Many of them are charming buildings, such as Ingestre in Staffordshire (possibly by Wren himself), Gayhurst in Buckinghamshire, and Great Witley in Worcestershire.

In the new countries, like America, the churches were of course Renaissance in design. In New England, for example, there are many beautiful ones of wood in the pattern of Wren's London churches, and very pretty they look, set on pleasant green lawns, and surrounded by timber-framed houses.

Pl. 23 shows such a church at Willen in North Buckinghamshire, not far from Newport Pagnell. The nave and tower were built by Dr. Richard Busby, Headmaster of Westminster School, about 1680, and it is now thought that Hooke, a collaborator of Wren, was the architect. The chambers at the side of the tower were added a few years later, and in one was housed the library presented by Dr. Busby. Both the outside of red brick and stone, and the inside, with the beautifully designed font and fine plasterwork, are thoroughly in the Wren manner, excepting only the apse, which was added in the nineteenth century. From the tower an avenue leads down to the road, across which is the Parsonage. One can almost see the fine figure of Dr. Busby pacing up the avenue, in his fine town clothes, to his fine town church, followed by the abashed yokels. Still Willen church fits its period, as all good architecture does, and perhaps the period was not a very spiritual one. Pepys was a great churchgoer, and a keen appreciator of a good sermon, though somewhat apt to have his attention distracted by the presence of a pretty woman in an adjoining

Founded on Belton House, Lincolnshire

Fig. 58.—Late Seventeenth-Century Dining-Room

Elizabethan Parlour. Pl. 10. Eighteenth-Century Interiors Figs. 99. 121

pew. He would have been quite at home in Willen, but not quite so happy in such a setting as Wing or Stewkley churches a few miles away. We give a full account of a country Greek classic church about a century later, in Vol. III, page 60. It is Ayot St. Lawrence, in Hertfordshire, and it also is not so very far off.

Fig. 58 shows a dining-room in a typical house, built at the beginning of William and Mary's reign. This room is a fine example of the work of the period. The walls are panelled in oak right up to the ceiling, and the latter is beautifully modelled in plaster. The carving is in the style of Grinling Gibbons, who did so much work for Wren.

Walls were not always panelled in wood. Evelyn has a note (1665): "Supped at my Lady Mordaunt's at Ashstead, where was a room hung with pintado, full of figures great and small, prettily representing sundry trades and occupations of the Indians with their habits" (pintado was printed cotton imported from the East Indies).

While we are writing about Wren and his work, we must take the opportunity of giving one of the love letters he wrote to Faith Coghill, who later was to become his wife. Surely it is a model of what such letters should be. Faith had dropped her watch in the water, and asked her lover to have it put in order.

"MADAM,—The artificer having never before mett with a drowned Watch, like an ignorant physician has been soe long about the cure that he hath made me very unquiet that your commands should be soe long deferred; however, I have sent the watch at last and envie the felicity of it, that it should be soe neer your side, and soe often enjoy your Eye, and be consulted by you how your Time shall passe while you employ your hand in your excellent workes. But have a care of it, for I put such a Spell into it that every Beating of the Ballance will tell you 'tis the pulse of my Heart which labours as much to serve you and more Trewly than the watch; for the watch I believe will sometimes lie, and sometimes perhaps be idle and unwilling to goe, having received so much injury by being drenched in that briny bath, that I dispair it should ever be a Trew Servant to you more. But as for me (unless you drown me too in my Teares) you may be confident I shall never cease to be, Your most affectionate, humble servant,

"CHR. WREN."

In a house in Guildford High Street

FIG. 59.—Scroll Staircase in Charles II's Reign

Sixteenth-Century Staircase, Fig. 26. Eighteenth-Century Staircase, Fig. 100

Now for the staircase. Once the designers had accustomed themselves to the wooden staircase, they rapidly altered and improved it in a variety of ways. The sixteenth-century type has two flights, side by side, and this construction is called "dog-legged," because the two flights together were supposed to follow the shape of a dog's leg. In the later seventeenth-century design we illustrate, Fig. 59, the flights are arranged round a central well-hole with a better result, but the constructional details are much the same. The balustrade, formed of a pierced and vigorously carved acanthus scroll, is very decorative. This pattern was never very general, but examples are to be found among others at Thorpe Hall, Peterborough, built by Webb about 1650–6, Durham Castle, a house at Eltham, Kent, about 1660, and particularly fine ones at Dunster Castle and Tythrop House, Oxfordshire, which are rather later in date.

The man on the staircase is worth noting, in that he is wearing a costume which came suddenly into fashion in the reign of Charles II, and as suddenly disappeared a very short time after. Evelyn speaks of it in his diary as "the Eastern or Persian fashion of dress"; and Pepys, in 1666, mentions it thus: "This day the King begins to put on his vest . . . being a long cassocke close to the body, of black cloth, and pinked with white silk under it and a coat over it, and the legs ruffled with black riband like a pigeon's leg . . . but it is a very fine and handsome garment." Again: "the Court is all full of vests." After this is an amusing little piece of gossip. Pepys says: "Mr. Batelier tells me the news, how the King of France hath, in defiance to the King of England, caused all his footmen to be put into vests, and that the noblemen of France will do the like." This was probably the cause of the costume being suddenly given up in England.

The seventeenth century was a splendid period for beautiful furniture, totally different in the later half from the Jacobean work of the earlier part. Leather carpets came into use and many chairs are now upholstered.

Our next illustration, Fig. 60, is of a bed, but we are not very sure that it looks like one. It was drawn in this way to show the great height, which was one of the seventeenth-century developments. The first upholstered beds started with square tops (following the lines of the oak cornices, as Fig. 27), with valances, and plumes of ostrich feathers at the angles. After Charles II cornices were added, and became very elaborate, then in Queen Anne's time designs became simpler. The one illustrated is of the time of William and Mary; the cornice of the tester, or top, and the pillow board are shaped in wood, and covered with damask or velvet glued on. The hangings were of figured velvets, or damasks of splendid pattern. The valances were edged at first with fringes, and then later with galon or braid. Head valances are those hanging from the tester; basses, those on the bed itself; bonegraces, the curtains over the head at the back of the bed; cantonnières closed the joint at the angles of the head valances. The colour schemes were very beautiful; blue and silver green and silver, rose and crimson damasks, olive green and rose on a cream ground.

Fig. 60.—Bed of the Time of William and Mary
Sixteenth-Century Bed, Fig. 27
Eighteenth-Century Bed, Fig. 107

In Evelyn's diary, 1662, we find that "The Queen's bed was an embroidery of silver and crimson velvet, cost £8000, being a present made by the States of Holland. . . . The great looking-glass and toilet of beaten and massive gold was given by the Queen Mother." Pepys, in 1665, wrote: "Where though I lay the softest I ever did in my life, with a down bed, after the Danish manner upon me, yet I slept very ill." Another entry, in 1666, is interesting: "I home late to Sir W. Pen's (his neighbour), who did give me a bed, but without curtains or hangings, all being down. So here I went the first time into a naked bed." People really used the curtains, because the rooms were being made loftier and the fireplaces were smaller than in the earlier times, so they felt chilly.

The Dutch influence was very marked at this time, on architecture, dress, and furniture, and a good deal of the last was imported from Holland. Such a source must be looked for with the fine old walnut cabinet illustrated as Pl. 28.

We will now turn to another diary, which is not nearly so well known as Pepys', but very interesting because it gives the woman's point of view. Celia Fiennes was a lady who lived in the time of William and Mary, and journeyed up and down England on horseback. Like Pepys and Evelyn, she was consumed with curiosity, and fortunately for us wrote of all the everyday things she saw. Another thing to note is, that Celia was not at all interested in old houses. Haddon Hall and Penshurst are dismissed with a few words. What she liked was a nice new house, and she describes these as being of the "London mode."

She gives a note of Lord Chesterfield's house at Bradby, Leicestershire: "Ye front have something surpriseing in it; its all of free stone wch is dipt in oyle that adds a varnish to its Lustre."

The houses were beautifully furnished. Here are some notes of Lord Orfford's house near Newmarket: "The whole house is finely furnish'd with differing Coulld Damaske and velvets, some ffigured and others plaine, at Least 6 or 7 in all Richly made up after a new mode. In ye best drawing-roome was a very Rich hanging gold and silver and a Little scarlet, mostly tissue and brocade of gold and silver and border of green damaske round it; ye window Curtain ye same green damaske, and doore Curtains. There was no Looking glass but on ye

Chimney piece and just opposite in ye place a looking glass used to be was 4 pannells of glass in Length and 3 in breadth set together in ye wanscote." Other rooms were "well wanscoated and hung and there was ye finest Carv'd wood in fruitages, herbages, gumms, beasts, fowles, &c, very thinn and fine all in white wood with out paint or varnish." "There was a great flower pott Gilt Each side the chimney in the dineing Room for to sett trees in." Another house had a billiard table.

Celia must have been a practically minded woman, because she notes details of Baths and water supply. Sir John St. Barbe's house, between Southampton and Romsey, "into a backyard where is a Bathing house and other necessarys"— "There is a water house that by a Wheele Casts up the Water out of ye River just by, and fills ye pipes to Serve all ye house and to fill ye bason designed in the middle of the Garden with a spout in the middle."

At Chatsworth "there is a fine Grottoe all stone pavement Roofe and sides, this is design'd to supply all ye house with water besides severall ffanceyes to make diversion. Within this is a batheing roome, ye walls all with blew and white marble—the pavement mix'd, one stone white, another black, another of ye Red vaned marble. The bath is one Entire marble all white finely veined with blew and is made smooth, but had it been as finely pollish'd as some it would have been the finest marble that Could be seen. It was as deep as ones middle on the outside, and you went down steps into ye bath big enough for two people. At ye upper End are two Cocks to let in one hott, ye other Cold water to attemper it as persons please—the Windows are all private Glass."

How they heated the water we cannot say—probably in a large copper. Another amusing little note on the toilet is in a letter to Sir Ralph Verney in Paris asking him to inquire for "the little brushes for making clean of the teeth, most covered with sylver and some few with gold and sylver twiste, together with some petits bronettes (boxes) to put them in."

Mary Verney speaks also of wooden combs being held in great esteem in London.

Great attention was paid to the design of gardens, and these generally included some hydraulic jokes.

At Wilton, near Salisbury, there was a grotto in the garden "garnished with many fine ffigures of ye Goddesses, and about 2 yards off the doore is severall pipes in a line that with a sluce spoutts water up to wett the strangers—in the middle roome is a round table and a large Pipe in the midst, on which they put a Crown or Gun or a branch, and so yt spouts the water through ye Carvings and poynts all round ye roome at ye Artists pleasure to wet ye Company—there are figures at Each corner of ye roome that Can weep water on the beholders"; other devices brought rain from the roof. In smaller rooms water was contrived to bubble through pipes and imitate "ye melody of Nightingerlls and all sorts of birds," but when the curiosity of strangers was engaged and they moved into the room, they were drenched with water from another line of pipes. We like to think of the seventeenth-century folk standing round waiting for the joke to come off.

Celia first saw orange trees at Sir John St. Barbe's house near Southampton and again at the Earl of Chesterfield's house at Bradby, in Derbyshire. "Beyond this Garden is a Row of orange and Lemon trees set in ye ground, of a man's height and pretty big, full of flowers and some Large fruit almost Ripe: this has a pent house over it which is cover'd up very Close in the winter."

Here are some notes on food:

They ate coarse fish—"In this parke is severall ponds wch affords good ffish, as does ye moate and ye Trent, as trout, Eeles, tench, perch, etc., the largest perch I ever saw just Caught and dress'd immediately wch Eates in perfection."

"Charr ffish . . . wch they pott with sweete spices. They are as big as a small trout, Rather slenderer and ye skinn full of spotts, some Red Like the finns of a Perch and the inside flesh Looks as Red as any salmon if they are in season; their taste is very Rich and fatt tho' not so strong or Clogging as the Lamprys."

In Westmorland Celia saw oat clap bread being made. "They mix their flour with water, so soft as to rowle it in their hands into a ball, and then they have a board made round and something hollow in the middle"; the dough was clapped into this, and then "drive it to ye Edge in a Due proportion till drove as thinn as a paper and still they Clap it and drive it round, and then they have a plaite of iron same size with their Clap board, and so shove off the Cake on it and so set it on Coales and bake it; then Enough on one side they slide it off and put the other side . . . they have no other sort of bread unless at market towns."

This sounds good. In Cornwall she met West-Country tarts, which was an "apple pye with a Custard all on the top, its ye most acceptable entertainment it Could be made me. They scald their creame and milk in most parts of those Countrys, and so its a sort of Clouted Creame as we Call it, with a Little sugar and soe put on ye top of ye apple Pye. I was much pleased with my supper tho' not with the Custome of the Country wch is a universall smoking, both men, women, and children have all their pipes of tobacco in their mouths and soe sit round the fire smoking."

Here is an odd way to make soap. They burnt fern or bracken and then took the ashes "wch they make fine and Rowle them up in Balls and so sell them or use them all ye year for washing and scouring, and send much up to London."

Celia went to Tunbridge Wells to drink the water; and she bathed at Bath, and this is how she did it. There was a cross in the middle of one bath with seats round it for gentlemen, and round the wall were arches with seats for the ladies, with curtains in front. They all sat up to their necks in the water. There was a gallery around the top for the Company to come and view the proceedings. In the King's bath the water was hotter and you could have it pumped on you. If you did you wore a broad-brimmed hat. The ladies bathing wore garments, made large with great sleeves like a parson's gown, of a fine, stiff yellow canvas—"the water fills it up so that its borne off that your shape is not seen." The gentleman had drawers and waistcoats of the same material. To go out of the baths the ladies passed within a door and went up steps and let their canvas bathing clothes slip off; meanwhile their maids put "a garment of flannell made like a Nightgown with great sleeves over your head, and ye guides take ye taile and so pulls it on you Just as you rise ye steps, and yr other garment drops off so you are wrapped up in ye flannel and your nightgown on

ye top, and your slippers, and so you are set in chaire which
is brought into ye roome. Ye chaires you go in are a low seate
and with frames round and over yr head and all cover'd inside
and out with red bayes and a Curtaine drawn before of ye
same wch makes it Close and warme; then a couple of men
with staves takes and carryes you to your lodging and sets
you at yr bedside where you go to bed and lye and sweate
some tyme as you please." The illustration, Pl. 25, is from a
fine contemporary drawing in the British Museum a few
years before Celia's visit, and shows graphically the lively
scene.

One constant detail in Celia's diary is the badness of the
roads. The hard high roads of the Romans on which the legions
marched were so neglected that Watling Street is described as
being "deep heavy ground." Again, near Leicester was "very
deep bad roads . . . I was near 11 hours going but 25 mile."
Celia mentions that in Lancashire "they have one good thing
. . . that at all Cross wayes there are posts with hands pointing
to each road with ye names of ye great town or market towns
that it Leads to." This was not general, because in Derbyshire
Celia had to hire guides. Ordinary folk could not help you,
because they knew not above 2 or 3 miles from their home.

Where the roads were so bad, pack-horses (Pl. 26) were
used for the trade and industry, which was still very primitive
but beginning to develop. Here is the description of a coal
mine at Chesterfield in Derbyshire: "They make their mines
at ye Entrance Like a Well and so till they Come to ye Coale
then they digg all the Ground about where there is Coale and
set pillars to support it, and so bring it to ye well where by
a basket Like a hand barrow by Cords they pull it up—so
they Let down and up the miners with a Cord."

Kent and Sussex were still the Black Countries, and the
iron-ore found there was smelted with charcoal. There, as
Celia says, "when they have lighted ye fire for to Cast bells
or guns they must be Cautiously blowing, and ye mettle will
be apt to fall down on the nose of ye bellows and harden;
that if it be not still Cleared off, would quickly damn up the
fire and put it out."

Perhaps this trade led to the old proverb that "A yeoman
of Kent with one year's rent Could buy out ye Gentleman of

Wales and knight of Sscales and a Lord of ye North Country."

Celia tells us how tin was mined in Cornwall; fine flowered silks were woven in Canterbury, crapes, calamanco, and damasks in Norwich, serges in Exeter, stockings in Nottingham, paper in Kent, baize at Colchester.

She describes the manufacture of serge at Exeter. The yarn was spun by the spinners, who brought it to market and sold it to the weavers, who wove it on their own looms. They sold the woven serge to the fullers, who put it into the fulling mills. Here it was turned round and about by "huge notched timbers like great teeth" in vats of a mud made of fuller's earth, to remove the oil and grease. "When they are thus scour'd they drye them in racks strained out wch are as thick set one by another as will permitt ye dresses to pass between, and huge large fields occupy'd this way almost all the round the town wch is to the river side." The knots were then picked out, and the serge folded, with a paper between each fold, and put in a screw press, which had a coal fire on the top plate. Some serges were dyed, but those for London were white. This gives an excellent idea of how manufacture was carried on by a number of people, each working in their own workshops.

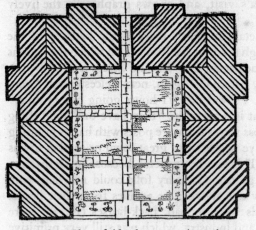

Fig. 61.—Plan of Almshouses at Amersham
(Plate 24)

Our quotations from the diary have been taken from *Through England on a Side Saddle* (The Diary of Celia Fiennes), by the Hon. Mrs. Griffiths: Field & Tuer, 1888.

Pl. 24 shows a very jolly group of almshouses at Amersham, Bucks, built by Sir William Drake during the Commonwealth. We do not know if Celia ever saw these in her travels, but if she had, we expect she would have considered the design rather old-fashioned. The flavour of Tudor times remains in the shape of the arched windows, and doors, and the gabled ends. Celia preferred a more full-blooded Renaissance treatment. At the dissolution of the Monasteries, many poor people, who had looked to the monks for support, were left stranded, so it became the fashion for pious people to build almshouses where the poor could find a harbour of refuge. There was something about the idea which stimulated the architects, because almshouses always seem to have been treated very successfully. Fig. 61 shows how the six cottages at Amersham were planned round the entrance courtyard.

We have written of the way that Willen church expresses the seventeenth-century character of its founders, almost as clearly as if we had met them in the flesh. In the same way a parallel could be drawn between architecture and music. When the architecture is twiddley, then the music follows suit, and both express their period. This is a point to be borne in mind. Unless we proceed in the future with more regard for beauty than we have since 1918, we shall be condemned as vandals —unless, of course, boys and girls determine on altering such a state of affairs.

Fig. 63 gives Dido's Lament, "When I am laid in earth" (from *Dido and Æneas*, Henry Purcell, 1658–1695), as a typical seventeenth-century song.

A great deal of care was given to the design of musical instruments.

Fig. 62 shows a spinet, or virginal, of the end of the seventeenth century; we see here the next development on the clavicytherium of the sixteenth century. This instrument has been laid down flat on its back, so that the family relationship to the harp is not so easy to trace. Played from a keyboard, the keys are balanced levers, having at the far end a jack, to which is attached a metal point, leather spine, or a quill, which plucks the strings as the jack is pressed up by the key.

FIG. 62.—Spinet, end of Seventeenth Century

Clavicytherium, Fig. 30.   Piano, Fig. 109

The spinet shown is separate from the stand on which it is
placed. Pepys wrote in 1666 about the Great Fire: "River full
of lighters and boats taking in goods, and I observed that
hardly one lighter or boat in three, that had the goods of a
house in, but there was a pair of virginalls in it."

Fig. 64 shows a gentleman playing a recorder with great
content. This was a whistle flute, or flageolet. Pepys wrote in
1666: "Being returned home, I find Greeting, the flageolet-
master, come, and teaching my wife; and I do think my wife
will take pleasure in it, and it will be easy for her, and pleasant."
Pepys was very fond of music. He writes of "my dear Mrs.
Knipp, with whom I sang, and in perfect pleasure I was to
hear her sing, and especially her little Scotch song of 'Barbary
Allen' "; and here is a pretty picture which reminds us that
the Thames in his day was nicer than it is now, and more

FIG. 63.—"When I am laid in Earth." Dido's Lament
By Henry Purcell (1658–1695)

Sixteenth-Century Song, Fig. 31.   Eighteenth-Century Song, Figs. 110, 111

I

used: "And so to the Cherry Garden and then by water singing finely to the Bridge, and there landed."

A great deal of information can be gathered from Pepys, of the sort of food people ate in Charles II's reign. On January 1, 1660, the diarist "Dined at home in the garret, where my wife dressed the remains of a turkey, and in the doing of it she burnt her hand"; but they went out to dinner on January 6, "only the venison pasty was palpable mutton, which was not handsome." On June 10, 1663, they went "to the whay house and drank a good deal of whay." September 8, 1663, "being washing day, we had good pie baked of a leg of mutton." At a banquet, "many were the tables, but none in the Hall but the Mayor's and the Lords of the Privy Council that had napkins or knives, which was very strange." On March 10, 1664: "To dinner with my wife to a good hog's harslet (from pig's inside), a piece of meat I love." On June 15, 1664: "Very merry we were with our pasty very well baked; and a good dish of roasted chickens, pease, lobsters, strawberries." Later on, "come W. Bowyer and dined with us; but strange to see how he could not endure onyons in sauce to lamb . . . and so was forced to make his dinner of an egg or two." "Hare pye" is said to be "very good meat," and fritters are mentioned on a Shrove Tuesday. They had asparagus; on April 19, 1667, the diarist went "home, having brought with me from Fenchurch Street a hundred of sparrow grass, cost 18d. We had them and a little bit of salmon—cost 3s."

In the diary of John Evelyn is given account of a great

Fig. 64.—Recorder, 1683

feast given by Charles II at the Banqueting-house at Whitehall to "all the Companions of the Order of the Garter." He describes it thus: "The King sat on an elevated throne at the upper end at a table alone; the Knights at a table on the right hand, reaching all the length of the room; over against them a cupboard of rich gilded plate; at the lower end, the music; on the balusters above, wind-music, trumpets, and kettledrums. The King was served by the lords and pensioners, who brought up the dishes. About the middle of the dinner, the Knights drank the King's health, then the King theirs, when the trumpets and music played and sounded, and the guns going off at the Tower. At the Banquet came in the Queen, and stood by the King's left hand, but did not sit. Then was the banqueting-stuff flung about the room profusely. In truth, the crowd was so great, that though I stayed all the supper the day before, I now stayed no longer than this sport began, for fear of disorder. The cheer was extraordinary, each Knight having forty dishes to his mess, piled up five or six high; the room hung with the richest tapestry."

Food was roasted, baked, or broiled; for the former the open fire would have been used, though coal was beginning to be burnt, probably in a long iron grate, or fire basket built up of iron bars. Before this would have stood the fire-dogs, or andirons, with attachments in which the spits could turn. The joints and poultry were trussed on to these spits, and there was a shallow tray under to take the drippings from basting, and the dripping we now have on bread, or hot toast, is so called because it did at one time drip into the pan. The spits were sometimes turned by a clever mechanical arrangement such as is illustrated in Fig. 65. This remarkable piece of smith's work dates from 1684. It was fixed on the outside of the chimney, and the spindle 5 went through the wall into the open space at the side over the fire. The spindle 1 had a squared end on to which was fitted a loose handle, this turned round a wooden drum 2, independently of 4, and wound up a heavy weight. When the winding was completed, the action was reversed, and by an ingenious stop, the drum at 2 turned the cogged-wheel 4 in an anticlockwise direction; this engaged with 6, which was connected by a spindle to the prettily pierced wheel in front, the cogs of which were cut on the bevel to engage with the worm on spindle 8; this latter had a small fly-wheel fitted at 9 which acted as a governor. At the end of spindle 5 was a wooden pulley, from which lines were taken to wheels on the ends of the spits underneath; this acted like belting in a modern factory, and the spits were turned round and round. Pots were suspended over the fire by cranes, one of which is shown on Pl. 38.

The baking was still done in a brick oven, in the way described in Chapter III, Vol. I. It is also usual to find in old kitchens provision made for cooking by charcoal. A sort of brick table was built up, with arches under it in which the charcoal was kept, and on the table little fires were made with this fuel, and enclosed in metal rings, and cooking was done over the same in small pots.

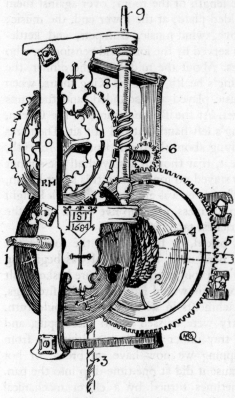

FIG. 65.—A Turnspit

Pepys was always trying to improve his house and make it look jolly; as he became more prosperous he bought a good deal of silver, and some of this was for use on the table. On September 9, 1664: "I out and bought some things; among others, a dozen of silver salts." "I this day putting my two flaggons upon my table." Later in the year Pepys pays "the

silver smith £22, 18s. for spoons, forks, and sugar-box." On
February 3, 1666: "Did carry home a silver drudger (*dragées*
—sugar plums) for my cupboard of plate, and did call for my
silver chafing-dishes." "Drinking glasses, a case of knives and
other things" were bought later in the year; and on December 31 the diarist tells us with great satisfaction: "One thing
I reckon remarkable in my own condition is, that I am come
to abound in good plate so as at all entertainments to be
served wholly with silver plates, having two dozen and a half."

Pepys' diary is interesting because of the little human
touches which make the characters in it live, and the diarist
gives us not only the noble thoughts suitable for publication,
but some of the mean ones as well. It is interesting to watch
his career, and in the end one follows his fortune with real
affection. In 1660, Mr. and Mrs. Pepys had only one maid,
Jane, but at the end of 1663, Jane, whose surname was Gentleman, had "Besse, our excellent good-natured cook-maid, and
Susan, a little girl" to keep her company. By September 1664
the household had been increased, and we are told: "Up and
to church in the best manner I have gone a good while—that
is to say, with my wife, and her woman Mercer, along with
us, and Tom my boy waiting on us." Pepys was a kindly man,
but did not hesitate to punish his servants if need be. On
February 19, 1665, we are told: "I fell mightily out and made
my wife . . . to beat our little girle, and then we shut her
doune into the cellar, and there she lay all night." Another
time: "Coming home, saw my door and hatch open, left so
by Luce our cookmaid, which so vexed me, that I did give
her a kick in our entry, and offered a blow at her, and was
seen doing so by Sir W. Pen's footboy, which did vex me to
the heart, because I know he will be telling their family of it."
The old ruffian had need to be ashamed of himself. But all
the maids would not put up with this. In 1666 there was one
of whom Pepys wrote: "Up and away goes Alice, our cook-
maid, a good servant whom we loved and did well by her,
and she an excellent servant, but would not bear being told
of any fault in the fewest and kindest words, and would go
away of her own accord, and after having given her mistress
warning fickly."

Pepys and his wife give us, as we have seen, a very clear and interesting picture of life in 1666 and of all the little domestic details that go to make up such a life, and as one reads, one feels that home management has altered little: certainly until after the reign of Queen Victoria, when women ruled their households and were expected to have cognisance of the smallest details, even as in the reign of Charles II. Our grandmothers we know filled large books with treasured recipes which had been passed down from mother to daughter or given as a great favour by some friend. Many of the recipes recounted in Pepys' diary are already known to us, but those of the wife of Oliver Cromwell, known as the Protectress, are less familiar. In the British Museum is a small book written after the death of Cromwell containing an account of his wife and his household, and the fashion of management therein. The book has been written in a vein of somewhat malicious gossip to expose the frugality and even parsimony of the household, but curiously enough the picture it gives us instead is that of a shrewd, sensible woman, who ruled her house wisely and well, and with an absence of waste very lacking in the profligate court life of 1664. The book speaks with horror of the herd of cows that were grazed in St. James's Park, although we are also led to believe that the resultant butter was excellent. Two of the recipes from her cooking book given here, and spoken of somewhat disparagingly as frugal and plain, appear nevertheless to our modern eyes as richer than we should wish at an ordinary meal.

They are as follows:

"TO MAKE GOOSEBERRY CREAM

"First boyl, or you may preserve your Gooseberries, then having a clear Cream boyled up and seasoned with old Cinamon, Nutmeg, Mace, Sugar, Rose-water and Eggs, dish it up, and when it is cold take up the Goosberries with a pin, and stick them on in rounds as thick as they can lye upon the said Cream, garnishing your Dish with them, and strow them over with the finest Sugar and serve them up."

PLATE 25

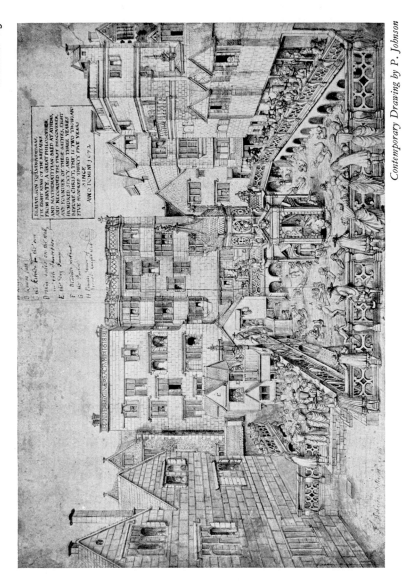

Contemporary Drawing by P. Johnson

The Baths at Bath, 1675

PLATE 26

A Pack Train

A Stage Waggon

Engravings by D. Loggan, 1675

A Coach and Four

Drawing by T. Rowlandson

Stage Waggon, showing Passengers

TRANSPORT, LATE SEVENTEENTH AND EIGHTEENTH CENTURIES

Sixteenth-Century Coach, Fig. 40. Seventeenth-Century Coach, Fig. 67.
Eighteenth-Century Vehicles, Figs. 115–19

"TO BROYL OYSTERS

"Take the biggest Oysters you can get, then take a little minced tyme, grated nutmeg, and grated bread, and a little salt, put this to the Oysters, then get some of the largest bottom shells and place them on the gridiron, and put two or three Oysters in each shell, then put some butter to them, and let them simmer on the fire till the liquor boils low, supplying it still with butter, when they are crisp feed them with white wine, and a little of their own liquor, with a little grated bread, nutmeg and minced tyme, but as much only as to relish it, so let it boyle up again, then add some drawn butter to thicken them, and dish them on a dish or plate, but if you have scollop shells it is the best way to broyl them in."

There was a great development in coach-building in the seventeenth century, and the Company of the Coach and Coach-Harness Makers was founded by Charles II in 1677. This points to improved roads and an increase in travelling. In Thrupp's *History of Coaches*, a very reasonable suggestion is made, that the coach invented at Kotze, in Hungary, in the fifteenth century was modelled on the German waggon, a sketch of which is given, Fig. 66. This very much resembles the English timber waggon of to-day. 1 is the front axle-tree bed, and 2 the futchels which go through it. The pole at 4 is connected to the front of the futchels, and has the drawing-bars attached to it. 3 is the sway-bar fixed on the ends of the futchels, and arranged to work under the perch 7. 6 is the transom, which is pivoted on the axle-tree bed under it. The

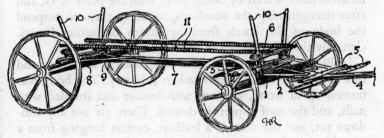

FIG. 66.—German Waggon

FIG. 67.—Seventeenth-Century Coach

Elizabethan Coach, Fig. 40. Other Seventeenth-Century Vehicles, Pl. 26.
Eighteenth-Century Vehicles, Figs. 115–119

perch 7 is securely fixed into transom 6. As the waggon turns, the horses pull pole 4 round, which by futchels 2 turn axle-tree bed 1 under transom 6, and the sway-bar 3 moves under perch 7. 8 is the back axle-tree bed, and the perch fixes into this, or, as in the case of the timber waggon, slides through it; the wings at 9 give greater security. This shows why the front wheels of a waggon are smaller than those in rear; they must be if you want a level perch. Standards at 10 were fixed into the transoms, and fir poles at 11 rested in between. Planks laid on these, and at the sides against the standards, made a very useful waggon. Mr. Thrupp thought the early coach-builders made a start by doing away with the poles at 11, and after strengthening the standards 10, using them to suspend the body of the coach from by means of leather braces. Certainly the latter were the first attempt at springing.

In Pl. 26 a coach of the time of Charles II is drawn, and this shows the coach suspended in this way. The body was framed up in wood, covered with leather and studded with nails, and the roof is prettily domed. There are not any windows yet, and the door is a leathern curtain hanging from a movable iron bar. The body of the coach is not unlike that of the sixteenth century, Fig. 40, but whereas that was mounted rather like a box on wheels, this one of the seventeenth century is a far more thoughtful production.

Fig. 67 shows a chariot such as Pepys might have selected. Chariots were smaller and lighter than coaches. He wrote in his diary on November 5, 1668, how he went to see his coachmaker, and "did pitch upon a little chariot, whose body was framed but not covered, it being very light, and will be very genteel and sober." In December he was "abroad with my wife, the first time that I ever rode in my own coach." The following April Pepys was "calling about my coach which hath been to the Coach-maker's to be painted and the window frames gilt again." So coaches had windows by this time. A few days later he found "my coach is silvered over, but no varnish yet laid. I stood by it till eight at night, and saw the painters varnish it, and it dries almost as fast as it can be laid on. I sent the same night my coach-man and horses to fetch the coach home."

And the next day was May Day, so Pepys went "at noon to dinner, and after through the town with

FIG. 68.—Lady's Winter Dress, 1664

our new liveries of serge, and the horses' manes and tails tied up with red ribbons, and new green rains," and doubtless old Pepys was very pleased with his gay turn-out.

In 1605 it was said that "coaches have increased with a mischief, and have ruined the trade of the waterman by hackney coaches, and now multiply more than ever." Another reminder of how much the Thames was used for communication is to be found in Evelyn's diary: "I was spectator of the most magnificent triumph that ever floated on the Thames, considering the innumerable boats and vessels, dressed and adorned with all imaginable pomp, but, above all the thrones, arches, pageants, and other representations, stately barges of the Lord Mayor and Companies, with various inventions, music, and peals of ordnance, both from the vessels and the shore, going to meet and conduct the new Queen from Hampton Court to Whitehall, at the first time of her coming to town. In my opinion it far exceeded all the Venetian Bucentoras, etc., on the Ascension, when they go to espouse the Adriatic. His Majesty and the Queen came in an antique-shaped open vessel, covered with a state or canopy, of cloth of gold, made in form of a cupola, supported with high Corinthian pillars, wreathed with flowers, festoons, and garlands. I was in our new-built vessel sailing amongst them."

Sedan chairs (Fig. 97 and Pl. 36) were in use in 1634, and Pepys writes in 1667 of "Sir John Winter, poor man! come in a sedan from the other end of the town."

Berlins were invented in 1660 at Berlin. They had two perches instead of one, and between these, from the front transom to the back axle-tree, two strong leather braces were stretched, going right under the coach body, and made adjustable by small windlasses, so that they could be slackened or tightened as desired. Experiments were made about this time in the use of springs.

As early as the end of the sixteenth century, long broad-wheeled waggons (Pl. 26) travelled between towns with goods and passengers, and were called "stages." Stage coaches began about 1640, and were like large private coaches. Outside passengers sat in a basket between the hind wheels, as shown in Hogarth's picture of the Inn Yard painted in 1730.

Illustration, Fig. 69, is of a library, dating from 1675, and designed by Sir Christopher Wren for Trinity College, Cambridge. In Vol. I, Chapter IV, a library was shown in which the books were chained to desks like long church lecterns, with a shelf underneath for the storage of additional volumes, but this was in the days before printing, when books were all hand-made, and very precious and scarce. When Caxton began work at Westminster in 1476, it was possible to bring out an edition of several books, instead of one at a time as

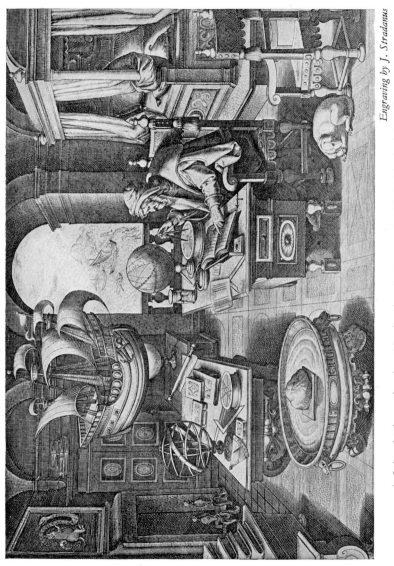

A Scientist investigating Navigation Instruments. Note Typical Interior

Engraving by J. Stradanus

PLATE 28

An old Walnut Cabinet, belonging to the Authors

Sixteenth-Century Furniture, Pls. 12, 13.   *Eighteenth-Century Furniture, Figs.* 101–7

Trinity College, Cambridge, by Wren

FIG. 69.—Seventeenth-Century Library

before, and this had its effect on storage. More shelves were added to the lecterns, and the effect was that of a double set of book shelves, back to back, with desks under them, and examples can be seen at Corpus Christi College, Oxford (1517), and Merton College, Oxford, and for a long time the books were still chained to the cases. The cases were placed down the room at right angles to the walls; there is generally a window at ordinary height between each set of cases, and a seat or bench. This is called the stall system, because stalls or compartments are formed between the cases. The library at Durham Cathedral is a late example of this type, and dates from the end of the seventeenth century, but shortly after this the chaining was done away with, there was then no longer any necessity to have the desk as a book-rest. Peter-house, Cambridge, 1641–48, and University Library, Cambridge, 1649–50, omitted this, and reached the limit of development possible to the stall system.

Wall cases had been set up in the Bodleian in 1612, and Wren combined these with stall cases, and raised his windows so that the two could range. He described his work in this way: "The disposition of the shelves, both along the walls and breaking out from the walls, must needes prove very convenient and gracefull, and the best way for the students will be to have a little square table in each celle with 2 chairs." Wren designed table, book-rest, and stools. The bookcases were panelled up in oak, and enlivened with carving in lime by Grinling Gibbons, The oblong panels in the ends are door fronts to small catalogue cupboards.

Wren used wall cases in the library at St. Paul's, with a delightful little gallery around to reach the higher shelves.

In the Pepysian Library, Magdalene College, Cambridge, are the bookcases old Pepys had made. He wrote in 1666: "Comes Simpson, the joyner, and he and I with great pains contriving presses to put my books up in"; and a little later: "Much pleased to-day with thoughts of gilding the backs of all my books alike, in all my new presses."

Together with this great new interest in books came another stage in the development of our civilisation, the desire to know why. Hitherto men had been content to do. Englishmen's brains had gone into their fingers, into tangible things that they could touch and feel, they were beginning even to construct mechanical things, minds were groping towards machinery. But now a new twist was given to life; in 1645 the nucleus of what was to become a very great society was formed. This consisted of a band of men who met together to discuss the new or experimental Philosophy. The seeds of this movement had been sown already by Leonardo da Vinci, Giordano Bruno, Galileo, and Francis Bacon, and the flower and fruit have been found in the Royal Society founded in 1660 and in all our modern scientific knowledge to-day.

From 1680 to 1682 Sir Christopher Wren was president, and the business of the meetings consisted of inquiries into phenomena, science, and of scientific experiments. One paper was read to prove that "small fossils be the result of the deluge" though Dr. Martin Lister contended in reply that they were "separate organisms fashioned on their own." Yet another member, a one-time president of the Society, read a paper to prove that "barnacles turned into birds." From such beginnings the Society moved slowly forward, and in the eighteenth century broke into two parts, those who were true scientists and those who became merely collectors of curiosities, and by the middle of the century this last was a very fashionable pastime. To house collections of "curiosities" Slater's and Tradescant's museums were formed. The latter was bequeathed by the younger Tradescant to Thomas Ashmole, who in turn bequeathed it in 1682 to the University of Oxford, and it became known as the Ashmolean Museum. The Tradescants were a remarkable botanical family who travelled far for rare plants; you can see a painting of a group in the Ashmolean galleries, and should visit their curious tomb in Lambeth churchyard. Pl. 27 shows a scientist in his study carrying out research on navigating instruments.

The seventeenth-century architects thoroughly appreciated smith-craft, and as there are several illustrations of ironwork in this part of our book, we think it may be of interest to give a few details of early methods of ironworking. Iron is found in many parts of England, but is most valuable nowadays when it can be mined with the coal which is used to smelt it, and this is the case in Yorkshire, Derbyshire, and Staffordshire. In the old days, before coal was used, the Weald of Sussex was the Black Country, and charcoal was used for smelting. The early workings were shallow, and abandoned as soon as the surface was worked out. The ore is found in many forms: in remote ages it may have been deposited by water, and is now described as sedimentary rock, being in reality rather like accumulated rust. The early process of smelting was a very simple one. A furnace was built up, and first was put a layer of charcoal, then another of iron ore, and then one of fuel, and so on. The blast was applied by bellows in much the same way as to a smith's fire to-day—in fact, a rough wall round the smith's fire would give an early blast furnace. A small quantity of malleable iron was produced in this way, which was hammered up into a "bloom." This iron was very pure and soft, and lent itself readily to hammering on the smith's anvil; the fault of modern iron is that being smelted by coal it is impregnated with sulphur, and becomes more brittle, and less ductile, than the old metal. It is this quality of iron of assimilating other materials which makes it so very useful to us; for instance, by adding carbon we turn it into steel, and increase its strength enormously. But to go back to our early smith: he had to forge all his work from the "bloom." Trip hammers seem to have been the next development to save the smith this trouble. These were worked by water-wheels, and the ponds which stored the water are still called hammer ponds in Sussex. The wheel turned an axle which had cams on it, rather like those on the cam shaft of a motor engine which lift the valves. It can easily be seen that if a large beam was pivoted at the centre, and had a heavy hammer attached at one end, it could at the other be raised, or depressed, by the action of cams. Pl. 39 shows such a hammer at work; though the scene is a century later the action is identical, and a friend tells us he has recently seen the device in operation in the Dolomites. This early application of power is a subject of the greatest interest, and boys and girls should bear in mind that until the steam engine came the millwright was dependent on wind or water.

A seventeenth-century writer indicates that the "bloom" was refined by heating and hammering, thus: "This they take out, and giving it a few strokes with their sledges, they carry it to a great weight hammer, raised likewise by the motion of a water-wheel, where applying it dexterously to the blows, they presently beat it out into a thick short square. This they put into the finery again, and, heating it red hot, they work it out under the same hammer till it comes into the shape of a bar in the middle with two square knobs at the ends."

Cast iron was produced by so improving the furnaces that the metal was much more liquefied, and could be run off into moulds, and this process makes it much harder than malleable iron, but more brittle. Cast iron was not much used in these early days except for cannon, shot, and fire backs. The

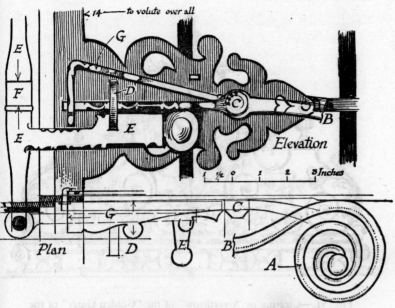

FIG. 70.—Espagnolette Bolt, from a house in Guildford High Street
(v. Fig. 59)

railings round St. Paul's, though, were made in this century.

Rolling-mills do not seem to have started before the beginning of the eighteenth century. Nowadays the equivalent of a "bloom" is brought to rollers cut to the shape of the pattern to be rolled. The white-hot ingot is put in on one side, and rolled through, coming out on the other roughly shaped, and of course longer. It is passed through the rollers, first from one side, and then the other, getting longer at each journey, until finally it is of the proper shape. Rolling-mills have to be big places, and the effect of one when work is in progress suggests the lower regions. The white-hot ingots and the iron bars or girders, rushing along the floor as they come through the rollers in all states of red heat, steam, and smoke, and men toiling and sweating at their task, all build up a picture which is very impressive. In this way are produced all the rolled steel joists, bars, angles, tees, and mouldings which are needed for everyday use, and which only need to be cut off to length

FIG. 71.—Cresting or "overthrow" of the "Golden Gates" of the Sanctuary, St. Paul's Cathedral, by Jean Tijou

for use. Not so did the seventeenth-century smith work; any bars that he could have bought would have been far too irregular to use in this way, and would have to be forged to shape.

This is a point which boys and girls should appreciate: the wonderful dexterity of these old craftsmen, and how with hammer, anvil, and chisel they were able to produce such pieces of work as we have illustrated.

Fig. 70 shows an espagnolette bolt dating from about the time of William and Mary, and made for a pair of iron casement windows. The scroll end A is really joined on to the lever arm at B, and turns on C, raising a catch at D, which so releases E. E is a short lever turning an upright bolt fastened to the other leaf of casement by F. At top and bottom of E are hooks which fasten this leaf to the frame. G is a spring which keeps the catch D in position over E, and so fastens the whole. The staircase of the same house is seen in Fig. 59.

In the design of iron gates, railings, balconies, and staircases the smiths of the later seventeenth century excelled, and

Engraving by T. Badeslade

The first Eaton Hall, Cheshire, close of the Seventeenth Century, with Ironwork by the Brothers Davies

PLATE 30

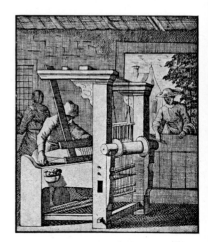

Late Seventeenth-Century Book of Crafts

The Wheelwright   The Weaver

Interior of a Glass-works, showing furnace, with Glass-
blowing, and Pack-carriers setting out

the craft experienced a transformation at the hands of the
brilliant Jean Tijou, probably a Huguenot refugee, whose work
at Hampton Court and St. Paul's Cathedral should be studied
for its glorious craftsmanship. An overthrow or cresting by
Jean Tijou is shown in Fig. 71.
But you can get much pleasure
in noticing the simple effective
ironwork in almost any
English country town. Other
celebrated smiths were Bakewell of Derby, Edney of
Bristol, and the brothers
Roberts from Wales. The
engraving of the first Eaton
Hall (Pl. 29) shows a magnificent curved forecourt screen
by the brothers; its gates,
altered and added to, still
survive in the park.

We have already mentioned
the establishment of the Vauxhall glassworks (p. 84), and
Pl. 30 takes you inside a glass
factory of the time, with a
furnace and blowers at work.
There are several jolly books
of trades of about 1680—
those by Van Vliet and the
one published by Otten—
where you can see workers

FIG. 72.—Pikeman, James I's Reign

making pottery or baskets, painting, printing, turning on
the pole-lathe, and busy on dozens of other pleasant crafts.
We hope you will like the weaver and wheelwright in the
carriage builder's shop which we have chosen for illustration (Pl. 30).

We can now turn from the arts of peace to those of war.
Illustrations Nos. 72 and 73 show a pikeman and a musketeer
of James I's reign. They are very similar to those of the
Elizabethan period.

The pikeman wears a helmet, breast and back plate with tassets covering the thigh, and this dress changed little until the reign of Charles II, when it was exchanged for a broad wide-awake hat with feathers, and a long skirted coat. Pikemen were always used in conjunction with musketeers to protect

the latter, when loading, from the charges of cavalry. These musketeers, when not actually firing, were an easy prey to the enemy. They were hopelessly cumbered with their heavy matchlock and rest, bandoliers, a powder-horn, a heavy pouch of bullets, a lighted rope match in their hands, and a sword girded at their side.

In Charles II's reign was invented a bayonet, which could be fixed on to the gun without stopping up the barrel, and this at once gave the musketeer a chance of offence, and

FIG. 73.—Musketeer, James I's Reign

defence, even when his gun was unloaded. Thus was sounded the death-knell of pikes, and, their principal function gone, they gradually from this time on disappeared from warfare.

Cartridges were also introduced containing the exact charge of powder and ball needed, making loading a far speedier matter, and superseding the heavy pouches of bullets and dangerous bandoliers.

These bandoliers were cylinders of some strong material, each fitted with the charge of powder needed to load the gun, and slung from a band across one shoulder.

Hand grenades and small explosive bombs came into use, and in Evelyn's diary we read that in 1667: "I went to Greenwich where his Majesty was trying divers grenadoes shot out of canon at the Castlehill, from the house in the Park; they brake not till they hit the mark, the forged ones brake not at all, but the cast ones very well." And again: "Now were brought into service a new sort of soldiers, called Grenadiers, who were dexterous in flinging hand grenadoes, every one having a pouch full; they had furr caps with coped crowns like Janizaries, which made them look very fierce, and some had long hoods hanging down behind, as we picture fools." "Their clothing being likewise piebald yellow and red."

An account of the dress of the new regiment formed by Charles II for the protection of his person, namely, the regiment of Life Guards, is interesting. It is thus described: "The privates wore round hats with broad brims, and a profusion of white feathers drooping over the hind part of the brim. They wore scarlet coats, richly ornamented with gold lace; sleeves wide, with a slash in front, and the lace lengthwise from the shoulder to the wrist; also white collars, which were very broad, and being turned over the vest, covered the neck, and spread over part of the shoulders. They wore scarlet sashes round the waist, tied behind, also large ruffles at the wrist, and long hair flowing over their shoulders. Their boots were of jacked leather, and came up to the middle of the thigh. Their defensive armour were cuirasses and iron head-pieces called 'potts'; their weapons, short carbines, pistols, swords, with a carbine belt suspended across the left shoulder. They rode long-tailed horses; on public occasions the tail was usually tied up, and together with the head and mane, decorated with a profusion of ribands." This description is taken from *The Historical Records of Life Guards*, and it will be noticed that the dress corresponds very nearly with the horseman in the beginning of the chapter.

It was in the reign of Charles II that provision was made at Chelsea for old soldiers broken in the wars. The existing building, known as the Royal Hospital, was designed by Sir Christopher Wren, and owed its inspiration to Sir Stephen Fox, who was Paymaster of the Forces after the Restoration.

Evelyn records in his diary in 1681: "Dined with Sir Stephen Fox, who proposed to me the purchasing of Chelsea College, which his Majesty had sometime since given to our Society (the Royal Society), and would now purchase it again to build an hospital, or infirmary for soldiers there."

The wheel-lock was the next development in firearms, and doubtless came about as a result of the many difficulties met with in using the matchlock. With the latter one can almost imagine apologies being made to the victim of the old-time gunner's displeasure, that he would not be kept waiting a moment, and then, when all the preparations were complete, and a final command given to the victim to look pleasant, the match would blow out and a new start have to be made. It is rather saddening to think of all the time, energy, and good work which has been spent in the world's history in the production of death-dealing instruments, so we leave the subject with pleasure and turn to country life.

After the restrictions of the Commonwealth, country sports and all kinds of hunting were followed with much zest and vigour. We have taken four subjects from Richard Blome's folio, *English Gentleman's Recreation* (1686), a grand old book you should see in a library; it is full of really delightful engravings by Francis Barlow and I. Collins. Our quartet (Pl. 31 and 32) is composed of stag, hare, and otter-hunting, and shooting—it looks rather funny to see the guns blazing away on horseback, by the by. In Blome's work are also shown, among others, fox hunting, fishing with rod and net, and plates of hawking for various birds, with accompanying dogs; it is, however, probable that this was on the wane. Horse races also started to be regularly run during Charles ii's reign, and Barlow has left us a lovely plate of the last race run before that king, near Windsor Palace.

A great deal of attention was given to agriculture in the seventeenth century, and judging by the number of country houses built then, both large and small, it must have been in a prosperous condition. The open field system, described in the last chapter, still existed side by side with farms which had been enclosed out of the demesne land. If the former was better for the labourer and cottager, the latter allowed the landlord and his tenant to adopt more progressive methods, and produce the surplus of food necessary for the increasing population of the towns. The enclosing was accompanied by much unfairness, but apparently had to be.

Good work was done at this time in draining the Fens, and we cannot now realise that this part of England in the seventeenth century was a real waste of water-logged marsh inhabited mainly by wild-fowl. Gentlemen adventurers undertook to do this work, on the condition that they were to receive a large part of the reclaimed land for their pains. The Fenmen, being Englishmen, hated improvements on principle, and during the Civil War broke down the embankments, with a result that much of the land reverted to bog. The Dutchman Sir Cornelius Vermuyden was largely responsible for the direction of the works, and struggled to final success through years of heartbreaking disappointments. You can see one of the great straight 40-foot drains, stretching for miles over the flats, that is still known as "Vermuyden's Eau." With grim humour Cromwell lent him some thousands of Dutch naval prisoners, with the idea doubtless that marsh draining was quite in their line.

Evelyn has a note in his diary in 1670: "Being arrived at some meres, we found Lord Wotton, and Sir John Kiviet about their draining-engines, having, it seems, undertaken to do wonders on a vast piece of marsh-ground they had hired of Sir Thomas Chicheley. They much pleased themselves with the hopes of a rich harvest of hemp and coleseed, which was the crop expected.

"Here we visited the engines and mills, both for wind and water, draining it through two rivers, or graffs, cut by hand, which went thwart one the other, discharging the water into the sea."

Evelyn was a great gardener, and wrote on this and farming. His book *Sylva* has interesting descriptions of early machinery; there is a primitive type of saw-mill driven by a water-wheel, and a boring and shaping machine for making wooden drain-pipes.

In Worlidge's *Systema Agriculturæ*, 1669, an illustration is given of a four-wheeled horse-drawn drill for sowing, which cut a furrow and sowed the seed in one operation, so that "one horse and man may work the instrument, and sow land as fast as, or faster than, six horses can plough."

Lord Sandwich presented Evelyn with a sembrador brought out of Spain—a wonderful engine, ploughing, sowing, and harrowing at once.

Another book, *England's Improvement*, was written by Captain Walter Blith about the time of Cromwell. He mentions the double-wheeled plough; the single-wheeled plough and

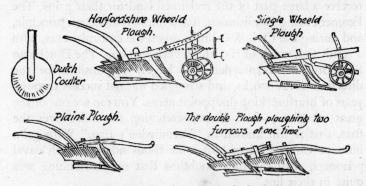

FIG. 74.—Ploughs, from *England's Improvement*
Eighteenth Century, Fig. 89

the foot-plough; the simple plain plough and a Dutch one, as being the typical ones in use. We have reproduced his illustration in Fig. 74. When one bears in mind how much the plough has meant to man, it is extraordinary how little attention has been paid to it; we do not know of any book on the plough. We remember that in that fine film, "The Covered Waggon," ploughs were slung underneath the waggons of the pioneers. With them they broke up the prairie in their new settlements and so gained a living for themselves.

Writing of agriculture gives us the opportunity of illustrating the next important development in windmills. All the mills we have shown as yet have been of the post-mill variety, the whole mill balanced, and turning, on a central post. The one shown in Fig. 75 is quite different. The old millers probably began to find that it was rather a nuisance to have to do one's

FIG. 75.—A Smock Mill

Post Mill, Fig. 23. Tower Mill, Fig. 93. Handmill, Fig. 94

135

work in such a movable workshop, yet they were confronted with the problem that the sails to turn must face the wind. This is how they overcame the difficulty. The octagonal body of the mill was constructed as a fixture below the head. The top of the octagon was finished with a circular curb, having strong wooden cogs projecting out of its circumference. The head being framed up separately, was arranged to slide round on the top of the curb. The head and sails were turned into the wind by the little vane at the back. From the spindle of this vane a pair of bevel gears operated a vertical rod, which at its lower end had another pair of bevel gears; these turned a horizontal shaft with a worm cut on it engaging with the cogs on the side of the curb. If the wind changed and the main sails went out of operation, the vane commenced to work, and the worm gear attached to the head of mill, wormed its way along the cogs on the curb and turned the whole head round. When the main sails got into the wind again then the vane stopped. The chain hanging down operated an iron rod, which passed right through the centre of the main shaft and opened and shut the louvres on the sails—a really triumphant piece of work, to bore so long a hole by hand quite truly.

The old millers have amusing names for the parts of a mill: the large cog wheel on the main shaft next the sails is the brake wheel, and this engages with one called the wallowers. The one immediately under it, by means of gears, operate a sack hoist. The wheel under again is called the spur wheel, and this engages others called stone nuts, which turn the stones. The corn being hoisted up is emptied into the bins shown by dotted lines, and finds its way by gravity through shoots to the stones, and the slope of these is adjustable to suit different grains. Peas, for instance, will require a different angle to wheat.

The octagonal body is constructed of timber framing on a brick foundation, and because the timber framing was covered with boarding and generally painted white, this type is called a smock mill, because the white makes it look as if the mill had a smock on. The little gallery around is a pretty feature, and the old millwrights knew how to do their work, so that it formed a pleasant addition to the countryside.

Now we can find out how the people amused themselves. Pepys was a great playgoer; then there were the Court masques.

There were no very great developments in the building of theatres at the beginning of the seventeenth century. There were very bad plagues in London in 1603 and 1625, the years that James I and Charles I came to the throne, and theatres had to be shut up, because it was feared that people coming together to see the plays would spread infection. James I issued a licence that the Boar's Head and Curtain Theatres would re-open "as soon as the plague decreases to thirty deaths per week in London." In Charles I's time six playhouses were allowed in town —the Blackfriars Company, His Majesty's Servants, "The Bull," "Playhouse," "Fortune," "Globe," and "Cockpit," in Drury Lane. But times were troublous, or perhaps too close and overshadowed by those of Shakespeare. Theatres were shut up by the Puritans in

FIG. 76.—Viola-da-Gamba, 1669

the time of the Commonwealth as being evil places, except the "Red Bull," which was allowed to give performances of "drolls," rope-dancing, etc.

At the Restoration a company of players started again at the "Red Bull," and eventually the old players came together again and two companies were formed: one called themselves the King's House, and the other the Duke's Theatre. The Duke's Theatre in Little Lincoln's Inn Fields was opened in 1662, and is supposed to have been designed by Sir Christopher Wren; it was here that Charles II went for the first time to see

FIG. 77.—Seventeenth-Century Theatre

Elizabethan "Plaie" House, Fig. 37.   Eighteenth-Century Theatre and Circus,
Fig. 122

138

a play after coming to the throne. Compared with modern theatres it was very small, but then in these days not so many people went to see plays. Our drawing, Fig. 77, has been made from an old print, and it will be noticed that though the design is much more modern than that shown in the sixteenth century, there are still points of resemblance. Over the proscenium, or opening on to the stage, are shown openings which may have been boxes, or were put there in memory of the openings in the tower of the Elizabethan theatre, where the trumpeter was stationed to sound a note when the performance was starting. In the Duke's Theatre they may have been only painted representations, which afforded the decorator an opportunity to exercise his skill in perspective. This they were very fond of doing, suggesting on a wall or ceiling that you could look through into some other place by painting pictures of it. Evelyn has a note about "Mr. Povey's house in Lincoln's Inn Fields, where the perspective in his court excellently painted by Streater." Elaborate scenery was beginning to be used at the Duke's Theatre before this; a play was produced at the "Cockpit," entitled *The Cruelty of the Spaniards in Peru*, expressed by vocal and instrumental music and by art of perspective in scenes."

In the Duke's Theatre the body of the house appears to have been covered in with a flat ceiling, but in the Elizabethan the whole of the pit was open to the sky and only the stage was covered. Pepys has a note in 1664: "To the King's House and saw the *Silent Woman*. Before the play was done, it fell such a storm of hayle that we in the middle of the pit were fain to rise; and all the house in a disorder." The King's House was a new theatre, built in Drury Lane just after the Duke's, which in all probability it resembled; and from this note of Pepys we can assume that the ceiling had a central open space. The print from which our drawing has been made only shows the beginning of a flat ceiling just over the proscenium. For the rest of the interior of the Duke's Theatre, the old print shows three tiers of boxes as in the Elizabethan theatre, though the space on each side of the upper tier next the stage (not being in a good position for seeing) has been used for decorative painting. The drawing shows a scene from Elkannah

Settle's *Empress of Morocco*. Pepys has another note in 1667: "That the stage is now . . . more glorious than heretofore. Now, wax-candles, and many of them; then, not above 3 lbs. of tallow; now, all things civil, no rudeness anywhere; then, as in a bear-garden: then, two or three fiddlers; now, nine or ten of the best: then, nothing but rushes upon the ground and everything else mean; now, all otherwise."

This note is of interest, because, as we saw in the sixteenth century, the Elizabethan theatre did resemble a bear-garden very closely, but in Pepys' time was being greatly improved.

The masque was very popular with the Court of James 1, and his Queen, Anne, is supposed to have preferred them to acting. Masques were spectacles rather than plays, and depended more on music, dancing, and transformation scenes than plot. In the *Masque of Blackness* given on Twelfth Night, 1606, the Queen and Court appeared with faces and arms blacked as Ethiopians; in the *Masque of Beauty*, an island was shown floating on water with beautiful effects of lighting. Inigo Jones the architect was employed to stage these performances, and made a great reputation by inventing the machinery which was necessary to effect the transformation scenes. Ben Jonson supplied the idea, and book of the words, and, alas! quarrelled with Jones, thinking that he obtained more than his fair share of credit. Jonson wrote plays as well, and in his time played many parts. He was undoubtedly quarrelsome, but a man of great genius. He started life as a bricklayer, served in the army in Flanders, and on his return became actor and playwright, probably at the "Curtain" in Shoreditch, and then with Henslowe at the "Rose" in Bankside. Here he quarrelled with another actor, and fighting a duel killed his man. Henslowe wrote to Alleyne: "Since you were with me I have lost one of my company which hurteth me greatly, that is Gabriel, for he is slain in Hoxton Fields by the hands of Benjamin Jonson, bricklayer." Jonson in consequence found himself in gaol, and narrowly escaped hanging. He beat Marston, a fellow-dramatist, took his pistol from him, and wrote an epigram about it:

"Playwright, convict of public wrongs to men,
Takes private beatings, and begins again.
Two kinds of valour he doth show at once:
Active in's brain, and passive in his bones."

About 1604 and 1605 Jonson wrote a comedy with Chapman, which was supposed to contain reflections on the Scots, and again he was in prison, and in danger of having ears and nose split.

Jonson was a friend of Shakespeare, and together they used to go to the Mermaid Tavern and indulge in wit combats. The tavern was the club-house of the day.

"But that which most doth take my muse and me,
Is a pure cup of rich Canary wine,
Which is the 'Mermaid's' now, but shall be mine."

And here is another line of Jonson's:

"At Bread-street's 'Mermaid,' having dined, and merry,
Proposed to go to Holborn in a wherry."

The Devil Tavern in Fleet Street was another of his haunts, and as well he founded the Apollo Club, of which Herrick was a member. Jonson fell into poverty, and at his death was buried in Westminster Abbey, and on the stone above, Sir John Young paid a man 1s. 6d. to cut this brief epitaph, "O rare Ben Jonson."

Coffee was introduced about this time, and Pepys has a note in 1660: "To the coffee-house (Miles'), where were a great confluence of gentlemen; . . . where admirable discourse till 9 at night." Chocolate was advertised in 1657 as "an excellent West India Drink," and tea in 1658 as "China Drink." See Pl. 34 for a coffee-house interior.

The illustration No. 78 shows some of the mummers in a morris dance. One always feels that this dance really was part and parcel of the Elizabethan and Stuart times. It was certainly in existence in England in the fifteenth century, but without the same hold that it gained later. Its origin is believed to have been in the East among the Moors. Morris dances took place at weddings on Holy Thursday, and at the Whitsun Ales

FIG. 78.—Morris Dance

Sixteenth-Century Game, Fig. 45.   Eighteenth-Century Game, Fig. 123

and Bride Ales, and a kind of pageant or play was also held, called *The Lord of Misrule.*

An amusing account is given by an Elizabethan writer of this ceremony. He tells how the Lord of Misrule is chosen by his fellows, how he is crowned, and then chooses others to be his bodyguard. Each follower wears a livery of yellow or green or some light colour, and they are bedecked with scarves, ribbons, laces, and gold rings and precious stones and jewels. On their legs are bands of either twenty or forty bells. They carry rich handkerchiefs in their hands or across their shoulders. The whole company includes drummers, pipers, dragons, hobby horses, and other "antiques." They all march to the church; "their pypers pypyng, their drummers thundering, their stumpes dauncing, their belles jyngling, their handkerchiefs fluttering about their heads like madde men, their hobbie horses and other monsters skirmishing amongst the throng, and in this sorte they goe to the church." They dance into the church and out again, and finally feast in booths set up by the churchyard. The people around give them "some bread, some good ale, some new cheese, some olde cheese, some custardes, some cracknels, some cakes, some flaunes, some tartes, some creame, some meat, some one thing and some another." Thus they banquet and dance all day, and perchance all night also.

The characters in a morris dance varied. The most usual were Robin Hood, Little John, Friar Tuck, Maid Marian, the Queen of the May, the fool, the piper, and several other dancers, also there was often a hobby horse and a dragon. The character of Maid Marian was taken by a boy, and the number of performers varied very much. The fool usually carried a ladle to hold alms, with a bladder attached, and a fox's brush on the tail of his tunic. Bells and handkerchiefs were always used.

In the churchwarden's accounts in Kingston is a note of morris dancers' dress in the reign of Henry VIII. They were dressed in gilt leather and silver paper, and sometimes in coats of white spangled fustian. They had purses at their girdles, and garters with bells attached. Sometimes bells were jingled in the hand or fastened to the arms and wrists.

Morris dancing continued until the end of the eighteenth century.

May Day was always kept as a holiday, with May Day games, morris dancing, and dancing round the maypole. Some say that the May Day revelry had its origin in the Roman "Floralia." In the poems of Herrick in 1648 are many charming references to May Day. In his poem "Corinna's going a-Maying" he speaks of the custom of placing boughs of may over each door:

> "Each Porch, each doore, ere this,
> An Arke a Tabernacle is
> Made up of white-thorn neatly enterwove,
> As if here were those cooler shades of love."

And again:

> "A deale of Youth, ere this, is come
> Back, and with White-thorn laden home.
> Some have dispatcht their Cakes and Creame,
> Before that we have left to dreame."

Candlemas Day, or the Feast of the Purification of the Virgin Mary, held on 2nd February, was usually marked by some revelry; and in Evelyn's diary he speaks of a masque taking place. Herrick tells of a quaint superstition in connection with the eve of Candlemas:

"Down with the Rosemary, and so
Down with the Baies and Misletoe;
Down with the Holly, Ivie, all,
Wherewith ye drest the Christmas Hall:
That so the superstitious find
No one least Branch there left behind:
For look, how many leaves there be
Neglected there (maids trust to me)
So many Goblins you shall see."

Fairs were still held, and Evelyn mentions both Bartholomew's Fair and Our Lady Fair at Southwark. At each of these he saw juggling, and performing animals. He also speaks of seeing an Italian puppet show in a booth at Charing Cross. He does not say if this was a Punch and Judy show, but they were certainly introduced into England about this time, as were also marionettes and dancing dolls. Jugglers, acrobats, fire-eaters, and other performers were often hired to entertain people at private houses after a dinner or supper party.

Evelyn writes thus of such an entertainment: "He devoured brimstone on glowing coals before us, chewing and swallowing them; he melted a beer-glass and eat it quite up; then, taking a live coal on his tongue, he put on it a raw oyster; the coal was blown on with bellows till it flamed and sparkled in his mouth, and so remained till the oyster gaped and was quite boiled. Then he melted pitch and wax with sulphur, which he drank down, as it flamed; I saw't flaming in his mouth a good while; with divers other prodigious feats."

Billiards is mentioned in the diary, and skating also, skate blades having been introduced into England by Royalists returning from exile in Holland.

Children's games were much the same as in the Elizabethan era, but a new system of education was started by a German named Komensky, which corresponds very nearly to the

PLATE 31

Otter-hunting

Shooting

Engraving by F. Barlow

Engraving by S. Gribelin

Elizabethan Hunting, Pl. 1, Figs. 34–6

PLATE 32

Engraving by F. Barlow

Hare-hunting

Engraving by I. Collins

Stag-hunting

FIG. 78A.—The Ostrich Inn, Wells-next-the-Sea, Norfolk

Froebel Kindergarten system of to-day. He advocated the teaching of children through their play to make clay models, coloured mats, and baskets with strips of bright paper; also to learn about various trades by means of action songs. Alphabetical bricks had been invented by Sir Hugh Platt in the reign of Elizabeth. Children's card games are often spoken of, and we read that grammatical card games were also introduced.

An interesting old seventeenth-century engraving is in existence, showing a primitive magic-lantern working, and it is described in a dictionary of 1719 as "a little optical machine which enables one to see in the dark, on a white wall, many spectres and frightful monsters of a sort that those who do not know the secret, believe it to be done by magic art." Scientific instrument making began in the shape of thermometers and barometers by P. Pastonelli in Leather Lane, and fire extinguishing engines in Cross Street in 1700.

A game called "Pale-maille" was played by men as well as by children. It was not unlike golf, only the ball, struck with a mallet or club, was driven through a hanging hoop. Charles II

and his courtiers practised pale-maille in St. James's Park, and
Pall Mall, as the name of the walk, has been retained ever since.

Having come to the end of our space, a tail-piece has been
drawn to show a characteristic piece of carving by Grinling
Gibbons. The great interest of his work is, that though at
first sight it seems to be a riot of exquisitely carved fruit and
flowers, in reality they are composed into beautiful designs.
His imitators emulate the skill of the under-cutting; they make
the fruit look as if it could be eaten, and the flowers picked,
but they generally entirely miss the grouping and composition.
If this woodcarving is examined, it will be seen that the masses
are carefully arranged and balanced, and that the lines of the
cornucopia on each side, with the eagle over, supply a framework which connects the whole together and gives relief to
the general richness. Without this design, the carving would
be only a beautiful riot of natural forms.

Grinling Gibbons' fine craftsmanship is accessible in abund-
ance at St. Paul's Cathedral—the choir stalls, bishop's throne,
and organ case; at St. James's, Piccadilly, and Hampton Court.
All boys and girls can go and study it if they like, and we hope
they will take advantage of the chance. Fine carving of a more
architectural type is found in the London city churches. Perhaps the finest room in London was the vestry of St. Lawrence,
Jewry, now alas destroyed by incendiary bombs, where the
woodcarving of large swags was in oak, with a well modelled
high-relief plaster ceiling and in the centre a painting by an
artist called Field. We can recall what it was like from
photographic records, as seen in Plate 33.

FIG. 79.—Seventeenth-Century Ornament

Sixteenth-Century Ornament, p. 79.   Eighteenth-Century Ornament, p. 215

FIG. 80.—Horseman, time of George II
Horseman, Tudor, Fig. 2.   Horseman, Restoration, Fig. 47

CHAPTER III

THE EIGHTEENTH CENTURY

WHEN the eighteenth century opened, the great question of the Sovereign's rights had already been settled. The Act of Rights, 1689, after stating the unlawful acts of James II, contained various provisions which ensured that Parliament must be consulted, and that it should be held frequently. To be quite sure that this should be so, it was provided that Parliament should vote the money necessary to carry on the country each year; so the King, if he was to pay the navy and army, had to call his Parliament together.

Dates	Kings and Queens of England and France.	Famous Men.	Great Events.	Principal Buildings.
1700 1702	Queen Anne, m. Prince George of Denmark	Duke of Marlborough b.	War with France	Castle Howard, Yorks, 1702-14
1703	. . . .			St. Katherine College Chap. Cambridge
1704		John Wood of Bath b.—A.	Battle of Blenheim. Capture of Gibraltar	
1705		Francis Boucher b.—P.		
1706		Benjamin Franklin b.	Battle of Ramillies	
1707		Fielding b.—W.	Union between England and Scotland	
1708			Battle of Oudenarde	
1709		Samuel Johnson b.—W.	Battle of Malplaquet	
1710				St. Paul's Cathedral finished
1711		Hume b.—W.	Archduke Charles made Emperor	
1712				
1713		Sterne b.—W.	Treaty of Utrecht	Easton Neston, Northants
1714	George I., m. Sophia	Gluck b.—M.		
1715	Dorothea of Zell	Sir Robert Walpole b.		Blenheim Palace, Oxford
1716	Louis XV. of France	Thomas Gray b.—Pt.		St. Mary-le-Strand
1717		David Garrick b.		
1718		Peg Woffington b.		
1720		Rev. Gilbert White b.—W.	South Sea Bubble	Seaton Delaval, Northumberla
1721		Smollett b.—W.		
1723		Sir Joshua Reynolds b.—P.		Houghton, Norfolk
1725		Greuze b.—P.		
1726		James Wolfe b. Robert Adam b.—A.		St. Martins in-the-Fields
1727	George II, m. Caroline	Gainsborough b.—P.		
1728	Brandenburg-Anspach			
1729		Goldsmith b.—W.		
1731		William Cowper b.—Pt.		
1732		Haydn b.—M.		
1733			Excise Bill	
1734		George Romney b.—P.		
1737				Radcliffe Library, Oxford, 1737
1740		James Boswell b.—W.		
1742			War of the Austrian Succession	Horse Guards, London
1743			Battle of Dettingen	
1745			Battle of Prestonpans	
1746			Battles of Falkirk and Culloden	
1747				Woburn Abbey, Beds
1748			Treaty of Aix-la-Chapelle	
1749		Goethe b.—W. Edward Jenner b.		
1750		Robert Clive		Prior Park, Bath
1751		Sheridan b.—W.		
1752		Chatterton b.—Pt. Frances Burney b.—W,		
1753		William Pitt		
1754				Holkham Hall, Norfolk
1756		Raeburn b.—P. Mozart b.—M.	Seven Years' War	
1757		Kemble b. Blake b.—Pt.	Battle of Plassey	
1758		Horatio Nelson b.		
1759		John Hoppner b.—P. Robert Burns b.—Pt.	Capture of Quebec. Battle of Minden	
1760	George III., m Charlotte of			Harewood House, Yorks
1761	Mecklenburg-Strelitz			Kedleston, Derbyshire
1762		Mrs. Jordan b.		
1763		Morland b.—P.	Peace of Paris	
1768				Adelphi Terrace
1769		George Washington		
1770		Beethoven b.—M. Wordsworth b.—Pt.	Ministry of Lord North and American War of Independence	
1771		Warren Hastings. Sir Walter Scott b.—W.;	Liberty of Press established	
1772		Coleridge b.—Pt.		Ely House, Dover Street
1774	Louis XVI. of France	Southey b.—Pt,		
1775		Turner b.—P. Jane Austen b.—W. Charles Lamb b.—W. W. S. Landor b.	Battles of Lexington and Bunker's Hill	
1776		John Constable b.—P.	Declaration of Independence	Somerset House, Strand
1777			Surrender of Burgoyne at Saratoga	
1778			French Alliance with America	
1779				
1780	?	Burke	Gordon Riots	Newgate Prison
1782				
1783		William Pitt the younger	Treaty of Versailles	
1784		Leigh Hunt b.—W.		
1785		Thomas de Quincey b.—W.		
1787		Edmund Kean b.		
1788		Lord Byron b.—Pt.		
1789	French Revolution		The Regency Bill. French Revolution	
1791				Custom House, Dublin
1792	Convention	Shelley b.—Pt.		
1793			Execution of Louis XVI. War with France	
1794			Victory off Ushant	
1795	The Directory	Keats b.—Pt. Carlyle b.—W.		
1796		Corot b.—P.		
1797		Schubert b.—M.	Battles of Cape St. Vincent and Camperdown	
1798		Thomas Hood b.—Pt.	Battle of the Nile	
1799	Napoleon Bonaparte First Consul			

A.=Architect. P.=Painter. Pt.=Poet. S.=Sculptor. W.=Writer. M.=Musician.

16th-Century Chart, facing p. 1. 17th-Century Chart, facing p. 81.

PLATE 33

St. Lawrence Jewry, by Sir Christopher Wren: interior of Vestry, with painted ceiling by Isaac Fuller the Younger; destroyed 1940

Painting by Peter Monamy

The old East India Wharf, London Bridge, *c.* 1710

PLATE 34

Engraving in "Vulgus Britannicus"

A Coffee-house Interior in the time of Queen Anne

The eighteenth century was a period of tremendous happenings. At home Great Britain was altered from an agricultural into an industrial country; abroad, there were great wars, which were to lay the foundations of our present empire. It is a period of history which is worthy of the closest study, because we are still feeling the effects of decisions which were arrived at then.

The Union with Scotland, in 1707, removed trading restrictions between England and Scotland, and this was the commencement of the commercial success of the Clyde, and of Glasgow's prosperity; ships sailed from that town to America and brought back tobacco.

The war with the American Colonies of 1775–82, was a sad and hopeless business. Among the Americans, the descendants of the Pilgrim Fathers, who had fled from tyranny and persecution, had little cause to love us, and the war afforded our old opponents, the French, an opportunity to aid the colonists in 1778. The treaty which acknowledged the independence of America was the Peace of Versailles, 1783, and this was followed by some ten years of peace.

Australia was visited by Captain Cook on his voyage of 1768–71, and colonists went there in 1787. This, with the conquest of

FIG. 81.—
Soldier, 1742

India, was to have great influence on shipping and trade. An idea of the scene when ships sailed from London Bridge to India can be got from Monamy's delightful painting (Pl. 33).

Then, as if the eighteenth century had not had enough of war already, the French Revolution of 1789 led up to the greatest war in which England had ever been involved, and which was to last for some twenty-two years and involve a whole continent. France presented the miraculous spectacle of a nation which, after apparently tearing itself into pieces by revolution and anarchy, became the greatest land power in Europe. The genius of Napoleon was such that it seemed as if all the nations must pass under his power, and this would have been the case but for our navy, and the sea power which Bonaparte could not break.

Holland was weak at this time, and, between the devil and the deep sea, lost to us her colonies of Ceylon and Cape of Good Hope. The battles of Cape St. Vincent, 1797, The Nile, 1798, and Copenhagen, 1801, led up to the short peace of 1802–3, and then came that great historic encounter, the battle of Trafalgar, of October 21, 1805, when Nelson met his death but preserved our liberty. This battle formed the turning-point of the long struggle, and made it possible for us to go to the support of Spain when attacked by Napoleon in 1808, and this campaign again led up to Waterloo in 1815.

FIG. 82.—
Soldier, 1742

We have gone into the detail of these wars and rumours of wars in the eighteenth century, because we think it may lead to a clearer understanding on other points. The wars gained us great additions to our empire, and so extended trade and the supply of raw material on which it exists. This stimulated industry, and its handmaid invention; we shall see later what developments there were in this direction. This growth of industrialism shifted large masses of people from country to town, to supply the labour for the new mills, and yet the wars, at the same time, confronted the country with the necessity of raising armies and large quantities of food-stuffs to feed the increasing population of the towns. Imports from the Continent were frequently stopped, and all this had a great effect on our system of farming and land-holding.

But to save being wearisome, we will now leave general conditions for a little and turn to the appearance of people. Here we shall find that the beginning of the eighteenth century saw the advent of the coat and waistcoat, such as are worn to-day. The long tunic and vest of Charles II's reign were changed gradually into a waisted coat, which was wide in the skirts and stiffened with whalebone to make it stand out. The

PLATE 35

Costume of the Eighteenth Century

Sixteenth-Century Costume, Pl. 4.   Seventeenth-Century Costume, Pl. 16

waistcoat, or vest, was still long and straight, and reached to the tops of the stockings, which were rolled over the breeches above the knee. The sleeves of the coat were still short, ending in wide cuffs, to show the full white shirt beneath.

The first man in our illustration, Pl. 35, is probably a country gentleman, and therefore his dress is sober, but a beau of the period was very ornate indeed: his coat was of silk, satin, or velvet, elaborately laced; a snuff-box lay in his pocket, with which he made great play; at his side a slender sword, and under his arm he carried a clouded amber cane. Cravats were still much the same shape, and although, after

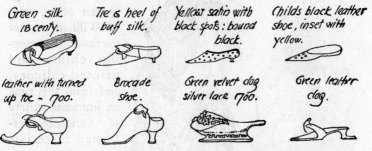

Green silk 18 centy.

Tie & heel of buff silk.

Yellow satin with black spots: bound black.

Childs black leather shoe, inset with yellow.

leather with turned up toe - 1700.

Brocade shoe.

Green velvet clog silver lace 1700.

Green leather clog.

FIG. 83.—Shoes from the Victoria and Albert Museum, South Kensington

the battle of Steinkirk, a black stock came into fashion, called the "Steinkirk," the general form remained unchanged. Wigs were usually tied in the nape of the neck, and were called "tie wigs," those for dress occasions being perfumed, powdered, and curled; three-cornered hats of dark felt were worn laced, but without feathers, these now being confined to the army only. While wigs were the mode, men's heads were close shaven beneath, and in the morning when they were at home it was the custom to wear instead of the wig a nightcap, or sometimes a turban, and a morning gown, or dressing-gown as we should now call it, often of beautiful material, and enriched with elaborate embroidery.

The second figure in the illustration, a young girl, is evidently not one of the fashionable throng. Her clothes are those of a well-to-do woman, possibly a squire's daughter,

and though of fine material and colour, they bear none of the
exaggerated details seen at the Court and in the world of
fashion. Her hair is dressed in ringlets, and is covered with
a little lace cap and a wide straw hat. A high wig was often
worn by ladies in town, with rows of curls above the forehead.
Skirts also were more elaborate at the Court, and were much
befrilled, and stretched out on hoops round the hips, with
panniers of the
material draped to
the back, and fall-
ing in a tail to the
hem of the dress.
Queen Mary, wife
of William III, set
the fashion for wear-
ing chintz and
printed calicoes,
and from this time
an immense variety
of variously pat-
terned materials
came into use.
Hooded cloaks were
still worn out of
doors, and ladies
went abroad in
muddy weather in

FIG. 84.—Bagnigge Wells, 1776

pattens and clogs. A very interesting collection of these can be
seen, together with shoes, in the Victoria and Albert Museum,
South Kensington, Fig. 83. Some of the pattens are covered
in leather, and some with velvet sewn with gold braid, and
often shoe and clog are made to match. As time went on,
hoops became larger and head-dresses smaller; in 1744, when
hoops reached their largest proportions, the hair was closely
dressed, and a little close-fitting cap was worn, often surmounted by a straw hat "à la bergère." This corresponded
with the "Watteau" period in France. But it did not last long,
the craze for artificiality grew, and ladies' head-dresses grew
in proportion. Greased, powdered, and curled, dressed high

Typical Figures and Scenes i

PLATE 37

reet in Eighteenth-Century London

over enormous cushions, and surmounted by imitation fruits, flowers, and even ships, the size of fashionable heads became so vast, that women were often compelled to travel in their sedan chairs with the roof open.

It is said that ladies were obliged to sleep in these erections, and at home in the daytime a large mob cap was worn over all, with ends that crossed beneath the chin, and tied at the back of the neck. Face patches were worn by all. Hoops were smaller, as will be seen in the second lady in the illustration, and ruching and pleating is much in evidence. On looking at the gentleman with her, we can see how coats have altered. Skirts gave place gradually to a tight coat, cut away into close-fitting tails. Knee breeches were fastened over the stockings below the knee, and shoes had red heels. We have not enough space to tell of all the different shapes of wigs and shoes that followed one another through the eighteenth century. They were many and varied, and shoes especially can be splendidly studied if a visit be made to the Victoria and Albert Museum, South Kensington, where also is a fine collection of costumes of the century.

In 1785 powder and mobs began to pall, and ladies affected curls and Leghorn hats, and the studied simplicity seen in Sir Joshua Reynolds' later portraits. Pantaloons, reaching to the middle of the calf, came in for men and striped silks were worn by them on dress occasions. Men's own hair was worn long, and Fox, who led the fashion, dressed in a more careless and negligent manner than had been seen before.

Horace Walpole in 1791 wrote: "I do not know the present generation by sight." Men "in their dirty shirts and shaggy hair have levelled nobility as much as the mobility in France have." A garment called the "Caroline wrapper" came into fashion, such as is seen on the last lady in our illustration— a garment still full in the skirts, but with the waist-line high, and tending slightly towards the classical form, which in the beginning of the nineteenth century became the rage.

In 1795 a tax on powder put an end to all powdered hair. Swords ceased to be worn, and men began to carry umbrellas! Thus ended the age of powder, patches, and brocade, and we can return to the doings of the navy.

FIG. 85.—The *Royal George*

Galley, Fig. 9. Galleon, Fig. 10. *Ark Royal*, Fig. 11.
Seventeenth-Century Ship, Fig. 53. Clipper, Fig. 86

We saw at the beginning of the chapter what a considerable part our sailors played at this time. Our illustration, Fig. 85, is of the *Royal George*, one of the famous ships of the eighteenth century. Mounting 100 guns, her tonnage was 2047 tons; the length of keel 143 feet 5½ inches; beam, 51 feet 9½ inches; depth, 21 feet 6 inches. Built at Woolwich, she was launched in 1756, the year before William Pitt was made War Minister, and sank at Spithead in 1782. The *Royal George* saw service under Admiral Hawke, and assisted in the defeat of the French at Belle Isle in 1759.

Starting with the hull of the ship, we can still trace the old galley beak head, that we have noted as characteristics of the sixteenth and seventeenth centuries, but this feature was soon to disappear, and Nelson's flagship, the *Victory*, built 1775, has bows which form part of the hull in modern fashion—a

PLATE 38

BUCKINGHAM HOUSE, ST. JAMES'S PARK   *Edward Dayes*

(*Size of original* 15½ × 25½ *inches.   Signed and dated* 1790.   *Engraved by S. D. Soiron,* 1793, *under the title of* "*Promenade in St. James's Park.*")

loss from the picturesque point of view, but an undoubted improvement structurally. The forecastle is marked, and the poop, but not in so pronounced a fashion as before. The three poop lanterns, with another in the main-top, gave by night the sign of a flag officer's ship. So far as rigging is concerned, the *Royal George* has a sprit-sail under the bowsprit, but the sprit topmast and sail has gone, and the jackstaff takes its place for the Union Jack. Triangular head-sails were also in use by this time, and by the middle of the eighteenth century stay-sails, on the stays between the masts, were common. The sailing diagram in the sixteenth century (Fig. 8) explained the uses of these, and how they held the ship in the wind for a longer period in coming round.

We have in the drawing square sails on the foremast and mainmast, and on the mizzen we still have a lateen with square sails over. After this the lateen has an interesting development. First the fore part was cut off, turning it into a four-sided sail, then all the sail in front of the mast went, but the yard still projected. Then the yard in front was cut off, and by this time the sail had become the spanker, or driver. Then about 1840 the Americans put a square sail in front of the driver, which was called the cross jack. Head sails necessitated the jib-boom being added to the bowsprit, and the dolphin striker was placed underneath to embrace the whole and resist the strain of the head sails.

These were the ships which led up to those of Nelson's times, and great art and cunning was needed in their handling. At Trafalgar our sailors had to depend on guns with a range of only 400 to 600 yards, and they just lobbed shot at the French. We lost 1609 killed, wounded, and drowned, the French 4528, the Spaniards 2405, and no ships were sunk. Nowadays, the torpedo has a range of four to five sea miles. At the battle of Jutland, on May 31, 1916, which like Trafalgar was a turning-point in a great war, Beatty opened fire at about 18,500 yards, and the gunners fired at a smudge on the horizon they imagined to be the enemy.

There is an interesting note on the design of eighteenth-century ships, in the catalogue of the Naval and Marine Engineering Collection in the Science Museum at South

FIG. 86.—A Tea Clipper
Galley, Fig. 9.   Galleon, Fig. 10.   *Ark Royal*, Fig. 11.
Seventeenth-Century Ship, Fig. 53.   Eighteenth-Century Ship, Fig. 85

Kensington, where all mechanically-minded boys should go. "A great obstacle to progress was created in 1719 by the English Navy Board, who, satisfied with the performances of existing types of vessels, laid down a fixed scale of dimensions and tonnage for ships of each class, thus leaving no power with the designers of adapting the vessel's displacement to the increasing weight of armament and other changes. This remained in force for nearly a century, until the demonstrated superiority of French vessels of equal rating initiated a greatly improved scale of dimensions."

So standardisation spelt stagnation in the eighteenth century, as it still does to-day. The next illustration, Fig. 86, is of a tea clipper, dating from about the middle of the nineteenth century, so that properly speaking it is outside the period of the book. As, however, the clipper marked the final development and culmination of the sailing ship before steam came in, it was felt that it must be illustrated. The performances of these boats were really wonderful. Tea does not improve by

being at sea, so premiums were paid for speedy voyages, and
the boats were built to obtain this end. The trading ship before
this had been of a shorter and more tubby design, not more
than four times the beam in length; the clipper was five to
six, and the lines of the hull were as beautiful as those of a
modern yacht. The gracefully rising bows show that the boat
could sail into the wind. The clipper carried a tremendous
amount of canvas. Starting with the head-sails, we have three
of these, though sometimes four were carried, the lower being
the fore-topmast staysail, then inner, outer, and flying jib. The
jib-boom, braced with the dolphin striker underneath, is
shown in the sketch. The foremast and mainmast have their
foresail and mainsail, and these with the mizzen are well fitted
with topsails, top-gallants, and royals. At the stern there is the
driver, or spanker, the lineal descendant of the fifteenth-century
lateen. Staysails were fitted on the stays between the masts,
and studding-sails on booms projected from the yards of the
square sails. Thus we have the culmination of the art of sailing.
The clipper was good before the wind by reason of her
square sails, and could steal into the wind with the aid of her
head- and stay-sails and spanker. We illustrate the *Cutty Sark*
in Vol. III, Fig. 182, p. 211. Here to our great sorrow we say
good-bye to the sailing ship, and wish that our drawings had
been a little livelier.

In the beginning of the chapter we had so much to say
about soldiers, that before we advance too far it may be as
well to find out something of their weapons. The flintlock
was an English invention of the beginning of the seventeenth
century, and remained in use until superseded by the percussion
cap fired on a nipple, early in the nineteenth.

Having discussed war and empire, we can now turn to
industry and invention, which was to have so large an effect
on eighteenth-century people. We have already seen in the
preceding centuries how man was always striving, even with
musical instruments, to invent machines to do work instead
of working by hand, and until the eighteenth century he had
to depend on wind and water for his power. The eighteenth
century was to make steam the practical form of power, and
its use revolutionised industry.

It may be of interest if, before we discuss the development of the power loom, we describe the hand spinning-wheel. This beautiful little machine, see Fig. 87, was introduced in the sixteenth century, and took the place of spinning by a hand spindle as described in Chapter IV, Vol. I. The right foot, acting on a treadle, turned the wheel by the connecting-rod and cranked arm to the wheel axle. The wheel, by driving bands, turned a horizontal spindle, and it required a certain practice to turn the wheel regularly, and not allow it to reverse action. The spindle was fitted with a pair of wooden wings called

FIG. 87.—Spinning

fliers, and fitted with little wire hooks; there was a reel on the spindle, and a small grooved wooden wheel which took up the drive from the driving wheel. As to the method of spinning, the preparation of the carded wool was described in Vol. I. A short length of yarn, already spun from the wool, was threaded through the hollow end of the spindle, and passed out of a hole in the side; it was then threaded through the wire hooks in the fliers, and tied to the reel. The thread was wound on to the reel as it was turned by the wheel, and the twist which is necessary to make the yarn was given by

the action of the fliers. If a piece of darning wool is pulled
to pieces, it will be found to consist of many short hairs of
varying lengths, kept together by twisting. So in spinning,
some carded wool was put on a distaff placed on the wheel
framing, or a portion called a rolag was held in the hand,
and the art of spinning consisted in feeding out the wool, so
that a thread of even thickness was twisted by the action of
the fliers. String, rope, and all sorts of threads are made in
this way. There is a delightful little handbook called the *Story
of a Homespun Web*, by Mrs. Godfrey Blount, published by
J. M. Dent, which goes into full details. Knowing how yarn
used to be spun, we can now consider the various steps which
were taken in the eighteenth century to alter all this.

In the first half of the eighteenth century, the masters found
the yarn and gave the work out to the handloom weavers;
these men did their work at home, or in their own little
workshops, and though they had to work hard, had the
satisfaction of being their own masters. The yarn was made
by spinners, and it took ten spinners to keep one weaver at
work. Attempts were made to remedy this, and in 1764
Hargreaves invented the spinning jenny; this consisted of a
horizontal fly-wheel, which drove as many as eight vertical
spindles and fliers. The machine was worked by hand, and
enabled the spinner to keep pace with the weaver. Arkwright
still further improved spinning, and in 1779 Crompton perfected what was called a "mule," which, by incorporating the
good points of Hargreaves' jenny and Arkwright's machine,
made the spinner able to produce yarn faster than the weaver
could weave it. Side by side with the spinners, the weavers
were improving their looms, and it was Kay's invention of
the fly-shuttle which was the first step in the chain of invention,
because it at once doubled the weavers' output. Before this
date, the loom was worked as described in Chapter IV, Vol. I,
and the shuttle, with its weft, had been thrown by hand from
side to side through the warp; in the fly-shuttle this operation
was reproduced by a mechanical arrangement.

With the addition of the fly-shuttle, the loom remained as
before, until, in 1785, a clergyman, Cartwright by name, who,
until he visited Arkwright's mill had never seen a loom,

invented one worked by water power, and in 1789 Cartwright, who had set up a factory, installed a steam engine.

Primitive steam engines had been used since the end of the seventeenth century, notably Thomas Savery's of about 1700. It was a kind of steam vacuum pump with elliptical receivers, looking rather like a hydraulic ram, and was used for pumping water from mines. But it was James Watt, who started work in Glasgow in 1756, who finally perfected this form of power, about 1776. In 1777 he wrote to his partner, of a pumping engine he had fixed in Cornwall: "The velocity, violence, magnitude, and horrible noise of the engine give universal satisfaction to all beholders." The new form of power was rapidly applied during the close of the eighteenth century to flour, saw, and silk mills, and the reign of wind and water power was over. See the account in Vol. III.

We have seen how the wars of the eighteenth century added to our empire and developed trade. As our colonists went to the new countries they sent home raw materials, and took in exchange the goods manufactured from them. It was a time of great expansion, and speculation was rife. Many people saw the chance of making fortunes, and the pity was that in doing so they inflicted great hardship on others. This came about because of the upheaval consequent on the new machinery throwing out of employment many of the handicraftsmen, who were perhaps too old, or too conservative, to take to the new methods. We have seen how the old weavers did their work at home, and this was possible when they themselves supplied the power which worked the hand-looms, but it was impossible when the steam engine worked the power-loom. All the workmen then had to come to the factory where the power was; these were built without any regard for what are called "the amenities of existence." Cottages had to be built close to the mills, and as people were so anxious to get rich, they had not time to think about light and air, sunlight and health, so the squalid industrial town came into being, with all its problems affecting life and happiness. It was not until 1909 that the Government of that day brought in a Town Planning Act, which specified that such a state of affairs could no longer continue, and that "amenity,"

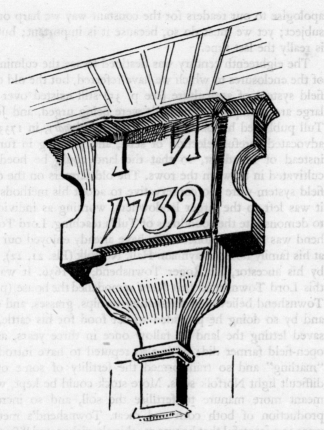

Fig. 88.—A Lead Rain-water Head, from Compton Wynyates,
Warwickshire

or the quality of being pleasant and agreeable, must be
considered in planning towns and building houses.

To revert to the eighteenth century, the many wars were a
drain on the man-power of the country, and at the same time
stopped imports from the Continent. The industrial developments drew men from the country to the new factories and
towns which were springing up, so that the farmers were
confronted with the problem of increasing the supply of
food-stuffs, with in all probability fewer men to help them.
All this brings us back to the land question again, and we

apologise to our readers for the constant way we harp on this subject; yet we must do so, because it is important; but this is really the last time.

The eighteenth century was destined to see the culmination of the enclosures to which we have referred, but the old open-field system of agriculture (see p. 35) still existed over very large areas. Improved methods were being urged, and Jethro Tull published his book, *Horse-Hoeing Husbandry*, in 1733. He advocated careful selection of seed, and planting in furrows instead of broadcast, so that the land could be hoed and cultivated in between the rows. The old farmers on the open-field system were too conservative to adopt his methods, and it was left to the larger landowners, working as individuals, to demonstrate the soundness of Tull's teaching. Lord Townshend was another pioneer. We have already enjoyed our peep at his family house, Raynham Hall, Norfolk (Pls. 21, 22), built by his ancestor, Sir Roger Townshend, in 1636. It was for this Lord Townshend that Kent remodelled the house (p. 96). Townshend believed in alternating turnips, grasses, and corn, and by so doing he provided winter food for his cattle, and saved letting the land lie fallow once in three years, as the open-field farmer did; he is also reputed to have introduced "marling" and so transformed the fertility of some of the difficult light Norfolk soils. More stock could be kept, which meant more manure to fertilise the soil, and so increased production of both corn and meat. Townshend's methods were so successful that he was mockingly nicknamed "Turnip," though it was soundly suggested that the term would be more fittingly applied to the heads of those who sneered at him.

Arthur Young (*b.* 1741, *d.* 1820), an advocate of enclosing, said of Townshend's work: "Thirty years ago it was an extensive heath, without tree or shrub, only a sheep walk to another farm. Such a number of carriages crossed it, that they would sometimes be a mile apart in pursuit of the best track. Now there is an excellent turnpike road, enclosed on each side with a good quick-set hedge, and the whole laid out in enclosures and cultivated on the Norfolk system in superior style. The whole is let at 15s. an acre, ten times the original value."

Young became the Secretary of the Board of Agriculture in 1793. He advocated reclaiming the wastes, breaking up commons, and doing away with the open-field system, and between 1793 and 1809 it is estimated that about 4½ million acres were added to cultivation in this way. The Napoleonic wars rendered such a course inevitable, and the open-field system was doomed when it was found that by enclosure the country could be fed, but great hardship was inflicted on the small copy-holders, who held a few acres in the common fields, with grazing rights on the commons and wastes. They led a healthy, interesting life, and were sturdy types. Too often their small holding was taken from them, as in More's words, by "coveyne and fraude," and they drifted into the towns to swell the volume of misery there, and to create new problems for later generations.

Bakewell, a Leicestershire farmer, born in 1725, greatly improved sheep and cattle breeding, and increased them in size and consequent production of meat.

Fig. 89 gives some of the eighteenth-century types of ploughs. Small, who made No. 2, established works in Berwickshire in 1763, and died about 1793. He was the first to invent a cast-iron turn furrow. No. 3 is interesting, because it was probably the first iron plough. Young, in his Agricultural Report on Suffolk in 1804, mentions a plough made of iron by a "very ingenious blacksmith of the name of Brand . . . no other in the kingdom equal to it." Brand died at the end of the eighteenth century. Nos. 1, 2, and 3 are all swing ploughs. The plough head was an important part of this implement, and the depth of the furrow was regulated by the position at which the pull was applied here, or by the ploughman lifting, or bearing, on the handles. The Rutland plough was of this swing type, with the addition of a land and furrow wheel at the end of the beam. The swing plough was more suitable for the use of the tenant-farmers to whom the land was let after the enclosures. In the old open-field system a much heavier plough could be used, and pulled by all the village oxen yoked together. There is much more in ploughing than at first meets the eye. The ploughman first measures out the field in strips a chain wide, by putting in sticks against each

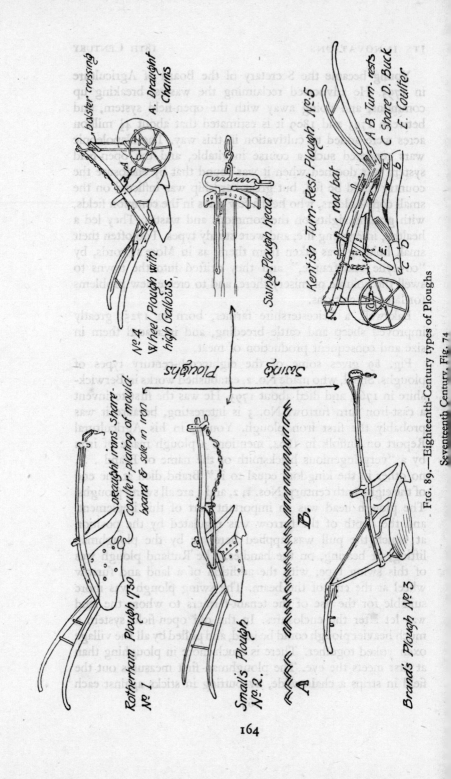

Fig. 89.—Eighteenth-Century types of Ploughs

Seventeenth Century, Fig. 74

A. Draught Chains
bolster crossing
Scissors

No.4
Wheel Plough with
high Gallows.

Swing-Plough head
rod bat

Kentish Turn-Rest Plough No.5
A.B. Turn-rests
C Share D. Buck
E. Coulter

Swing Ploughs

Rotherham Plough 1750
draught irons share-
coulter-plating of mould
board & sole in iron
No.1

Small's Plough
No.2.

A. B.

Brand's Plough No.3

164

hedgerow. By the way, remember that a chain is the length
of a cricket pitch, or 4 rods, which is the countryman's great
measure. The ploughman starts by ploughing from one stick
to another, and if he is a good man he keeps an absolutely
straight line. He does not plough the
next furrow immediately alongside the
first, because this would resolve itself
into a series of ridges as A, Fig. 89 ;
instead he proceeds along the hedgerow, and his path is called the headland,
and strikes the next furrow up from
the stick a chain away from the first.
In this way he produces the effect shown
in B, Fig. 89. The point where the
slices cut by the plough incline and
meet together is the ridge, and where
they part the furrow. These furrows
are used for drainage; on wet ground
they might be closer together than a
chain. Where ploughed land has been
put down to grass, you can still trace
the line of the old water furrows, and
in the late afternoon, with a low sun,
the field has a corrugated look to
remind you of the days when we still
grew corn, as we must again now.

No. 4, Fig. 89, is an interesting
type used in East Anglia. The set of
the plough was adjusted by the draught
chains.

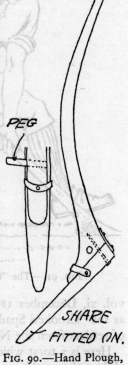

FIG. 90.—Hand Plough,
West Highlands

The Kentish Turn-Rest plough,
No. 5, was an exception to this rule,
and was designed to lay all the furrow slices in one
direction. This was very useful on the side of sloping
downs, and the plough went up and down and cut the furrow
slices side by side, without any journeys across the headlands.
It was arranged in this way. The turn-rest B was removable
and reversible, so at the end of the furrow it was taken off,
and put on the other side of the plough, and the coulter was

adjustable and kept in position by the rod bat. With this ploughing you did not get ridge and water furrows.

We are indebted to Messrs. Ransomes, Sims & Jefferies, of Ipswich, for recommending us to read *The Implements of Agriculture*, by J. Allen Ransome (Ridgeway), 1843, from which we gathered much of our information.

The last plough we are going to mention is the Hand plough, as Fig. 90, which was and still is used in the West Highlands. Fig. 91, which shows how the implement was used, was made from a sketch in *Harper*, vol. xi, December 1885–May 1886, and here it is described as the "Crooked Spade" used in Cape Breton by descendants of settlers from the North of Scotland.

FIG. 91.—The "Crooked Spade"

Here is a toast which brings in the plough and some sound philosophy at the same time:

"Let the wealthy and great
Roll in splendour and state,
I envy them not, I declare it;
I eat my own lamb,
My chickens and ham,
I shear my own fleece and I wear it.
I have lawns, I have bowers,
I have fruit, I have flowers,

166

The lark is my morning alarmer;
So my jolly boys now,
Here's God speed the plough,
Long life and success to the farmer."

You can often see verses like these with farming scenes pictured on amusing china mugs.

We read the other day in a paper that we import each year into England millions of yolks of eggs from China. These may be sold as "Farmyard," and the buyers may not know that the farm was in China. It is an awful thought, and we wish

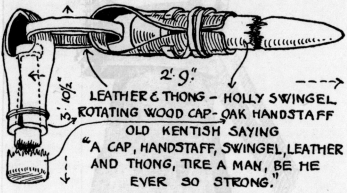

2' 9"
← 10½ →
13 →
LEATHER & THONG - HOLLY SWINGEL
ROTATING WOOD CAP - OAK HANDSTAFF
OLD KENTISH SAYING
"A CAP, HANDSTAFF, SWINGEL, LEATHER
AND THONG, TIRE A MAN, BE HE
EVER SO STRONG."

FIG. 92.—Details of Flail

the plough could be sped here in England once again, so that we could eat our own lambs, our chickens and ham, and eggs, instead of having to kill them off for lack of feeding stuffs.

After the corn was grown and reaped, it was carried to the barn and threshed with flails, as shown in Pl. 6. Jethro Tull (1730) is credited with having been the first to invent a threshing-machine, because he was "wicked enough to construct a machine which, by working a set of sticks, beat out the corn without manual labour." Fig. 92 gives the detail of the handstaff and swingel of the flail. Made by an old labourer with wood cut out of the hedgerow, his jack knife, and an old boot, it is a clever anticipation of a universal joint.

Writing of agriculture affords us the opportunity to illustrate the last of our windmills, Fig. 93, and we think it is a beauty. This type was called the tower mill, and its mechanism

FIG. 93.—A Tower Mill

Post Mill, Fig. 23.   Smock Mill, Fig. 75.   Handmill, Fig. 94

is the same as that described on page 136. This sketch shows
how the louvres to the sails are not all fixed in one and the
same plane. The louvres are shown open, but when closed

168

would form a nearly continuous surface, with a twist in each sail rather like that to the propeller of a steamer. If the drawing is examined, it will readily be seen that the wind acting on these sails would rotate them in an anti-clockwise direction. The brick tower is an extraordinarily fine piece of work. The lower plan is octagonal, with the external angles taken off, and in the upper stage is developed in a very simple way into a regular sixteen-sided figure. The old bricklayer who built this must have been a fine craftsman.

It is obvious that methods so successful as those of Townshend and Bakewell, if bad for the small owners, were very good for the landlords, and great fortunes were made. Land which could be let at ten times the original value meant greatly increased rent rolls, so we find that many very wonderful country houses were built at this time, some of them so large as to be more aptly described as palaces. Judged by plan, these are not interesting. The lay-out usually consisted of a central portion containing the reception rooms, with the stables in one wing, connected by a colonnade with the main building, and the kitchens in another. Such a house is described on p. 176 (also Pl. 29), and there is no evidence of any regard for the comfort of the servants, or hardly any recognition of them as fellow human beings; their part of the house was in the basement, and in one of Robert Adam's villas the kitchens are built in a pit, sunk in the ground at some little distance, and connected with the basement of the house by a subterranean tunnel. This plan clearly aimed at expressing the idea that servants, kitchens, and offices did not exist at all. So the eighteenth-century houses are not nearly so human or practical as those of Elizabeth's time, when difficulties were not dodged but grappled with. The keynote of the eighteenth-century house was display.

We emphasise these points, because this book may be read by boys and girls who will design houses later on, and to them we give reminder that architecture is a practical art: if they can arrange a house in which a family can live in comfort, into the rooms of which the sun will shine, and dirt and disease be kept away, they will have rendered good service; if they can do this, and add beauty as well, they will be great architects,

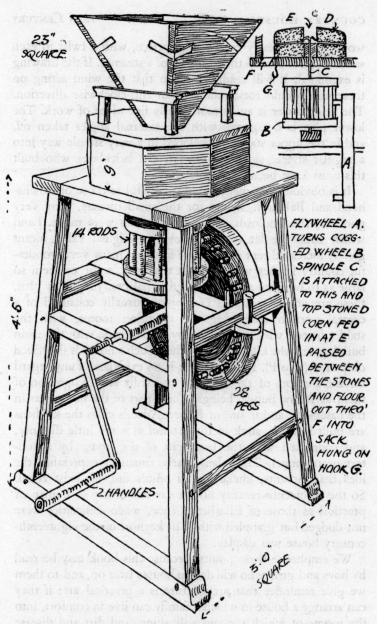

23" SQUARE

E D

F A

G C

B

A

9"

14 RODS

4:6"

FLYWHEEL A.
TURNS COGG-
-ED WHEEL B
SPINDLE C
IS ATTACHED
TO THIS AND
TOP STONE D
CORN FED
IN AT E
PASSED
BETWEEN
THE STONES
AND FLOUR
OUT THRO'
F INTO
SACK
HUNG ON
HOOK G.

28 PEGS

2 HANDLES.

3:0 SQUARE

FIG. 94.—Handmill from Long Crichel, Dorset, now in Pitt Rivers
Museum, Farnham, Dorset

Post Mill, Fig. 23.   Smock Mill, Fig. 75.   Tower Mill, Fig. 93.

but if they seek only the latter quality, then they will fail, as did the designers of the larger eighteenth-century houses.

It is perhaps the smaller houses which show the Georgian architects at their best—the pleasant old-fashioned places one finds to-day in almost any country town. The doctor generally lives in one; and the lawyer will have another. The walls are faced with red bricks that have weathered to a delightful mellowness; the sash windows are of pleasant proportions, disposed in a regular way. There is a good robust cornice, which provides a brim to the roof, and in the latter are dormer windows. The doorways are always interesting, and there may be some fine iron railings and gates. Internally the basement kitchen is generally avoided, and the rooms are planned for comfort rather than display. Walls

FIG. 95.—Bristol Ware

are pleasantly panelled, and the staircases good. They are eminently houses to live in.

Our illustration, Fig. 96, shows a house built in 1701, right at the beginning of the eighteenth century, and it may have been designed by Wren or one of his pupils; undoubtedly it was taken as a model for the other houses of this type to which we have just referred, though this particular one is built of stone. It is known as Mompesson House, and was for long the Judge's Lodging. Inside are some good interiors and a very fine staircase. In design this house is very simple

FIG. 96.—An early Eighteenth-Century House, in the Close, Salisbury

Timber-framed House, Fig. 15. Sixteenth-Century Stone House, Pl. 9.
Seventeenth-Century House, Pl. 21. Eighteenth-Century Town House, Fig. 97

and unpretentious, yet full of dignity. It is beautifully pro-
portioned, and the spacing of the windows is admirable. The
plain walling surfaces at the sides are used in contrast to the
richer treatment of door and window over, and the composition is bound together by the cornice. Across the whole front
is spun a web of beautiful wrought ironwork, which shows
against the stone like so much lace, and this has a just admixture
of richness and plainness. The roof is covered with red tiles,
and it should be noticed how the shape of the house is an
oblong, which can be covered with plain slopes, hipped at
the angles, without any gables. We saw in the Middle Ages
how the house started as a hall with a roof of its own, around
which were grouped the solar at one end and the kitchen at
the other, and the appearance was rather that of a collection
of buildings grouped together. Our present illustration shows
how in the course of centuries these all merged into one
building, under one roof.

The windows of the house should be noticed. Up till now we have only seen the casement variety, where the opening part, generally in iron, was hinged at the side like a door. In Fig. 96 we meet for the first time what are known as sash windows. Those at Raynham Hall (Pl. 21) were inserted about 1730, nearly a century after the house was built. The frames of these are hollow boxes used to conceal weights, which, with lines running over pulleys, counterbalance the sash. This type of window was not used in England until the end of the seventeenth century, but from a book called *A Journey to Paris*, published in 1698, we hear that they were regarded as an English invention. "The Marchal very obligingly showed us his own apartment, for all the rest of the house was full of workmen. He showed us his great sash windows; how easily they might be lifted up and down, and stood at any height, which contrivance he said he had out of England, by a small model brought on purpose from thence, there being nothing of this poise in windows in France before."

This window question had a great deal to do with the architectural appearance of houses. From Gothic times down to those of Elizabeth and James I, windows were formed by placing openings side by side, the stone or wood division between being called a mullion; sometimes they were divided in their height by horizontal transoms. It was a very useful type, because one could arrange windows to almost any size, by bringing the requisite number of openings or units together. The glazing was in small pieces of glass, leaded up either in plain oblongs, diamond-shaped lozenges, or pretty geometrical patterns. Inigo Jones does not seem to have troubled very much about the filling in and glazing of his windows, and used wooden frames and casement windows with lead glazing. Then came sash windows, in which the sashes were divided up by wooden bars, and this necessitated the use of larger sheets of glass than was the case with lead glazing. The French, though we gather that they experimented with these, never adopted them, and still use large casement windows generally opening inwards with a fanlight over. The old glass was blown, and has pleasant peculiarities. A blow-pipe was put into a crucible of molten glass (Pl. 30), and a sufficient quantity

Chandos House, Queen Anne Street, London, by Robert Adam, 1771

FIG. 97.—A Town House of the later Eighteenth Century

Timber-framed House, Fig. 15. Sixteenth-Century Stone House, Pl. 9.
Seventeenth-Century House, Pl. 21. Eighteenth-Century House, Fig. 96

brought out on the end; this was blown, and then the blow-
pipe was rapidly twisted round and round, with the result
that a large thin disc was formed at the end of the blow-pipe.
From the outer parts of this were cut the panes of glass for
the windows, and the centre where it had been attached to
the blow-pipe was thicker, and had a knot when broken off,
which formed the bull's-eye one sometimes sees in old windows. This old blown glass is not quite regular, but looks jolly
in use, and gives the house a lively appearance, because as one
walks past, the light is caught and reflected from the different
surfaces, which are not all in the same plane.

Fig. 97 shows a town house of about 1771, typical of the
work of Robert Adam the architect. The exteriors of his houses
were generally very simple, depending for effect on a skilful

disposition of well-proportioned windows; there might be a
string course at the level of the window sills, and the front
of the house was usually finished with a good cornice. The
small amount of ornament used was centred on the doorway.
In this case we have fluted columns of the "Doric" order, and
in the entablature over, the lower member called the architrave
has been omitted, with the result that the frieze rests directly
on the top member, or abacus, of the cap to the column. This
kind of ornament, and the graceful fanlight over the door,
are typical of Adam's work. The front railings should be
noticed, with the lantern holders, which were necessary before
the days of gas; on the standards which support these are
cone-shaped link-extinguishers. The link-boy, when he had
lighted you home, extinguished his link by pushing it up into
the cone. The chairmen, with their sedan, show a very usual
method of going about London in the eighteenth century.
We have drawn one in colour on plates 36 and 37, as part
of a typical street scene of mid eighteenth-century London,
on which Dr. Johnson appears. There is a public-house in
Mayfair, West London, still called *The Two Chairmen*; it used
to be frequented by upper class servants. There is another
called *The Running Footman*.

The eighteenth century was a great time for the amateur
architect. The Englishman who had been content to live on
his land in Elizabethan times, had for his descendants in the
eighteenth century men who did not feel that their education
was complete unless they had made the Grand Tour. They
came back from Italy full of contempt for their old homes,
and proceeded to dot about on the countryside exact reproduc-
tions of Italian villas. Practical considerations were abandoned,
and no house was thought fit to live in unless it followed the
rules laid down by Palladio. He was an Italian architect, born
in Vicenza in 1518, where he did most of his work, and died
in 1580. Architecture became an exact art, and a matter of
rule, and the amateur designed houses according to Palladio,
on the rules laid down in Gibb's *Book of Architecture*, 1728, or
Isaac Ware's *Compleat Body of Architecture*, 1756.

Lord Burlington was one of the amateurs, and a good tale
is told of a house he designed for General Wade, who,

apparently not finding it comfortable, was advised by Lord Chesterfield to take a house on the opposite side of the road and look at his own.

There is an interesting account of Buckingham House, built in 1705, which stood where Buckingham Palace now is, looking down the Mall. The house was bought by George III in 1762, and was known afterwards as the Queen's Palace. It had a central block, and side wings, connected with open colonnades. This is how the duke described his home and life: "I rise now in summer about seven o'clock, from a very large bed-chamber, entirely quiet, high, and free from the early sun, to walk in the gardens . . . my iron palisade that encompasses a square court, which has in the midst a great basin with statues and waterworks, and, from its entrance, rises all the way imperceptibly, till we mount to a terrace in front of the hall." At the sides of the court were two wings joined to the house "by corridores, supported by Ionic pillars. In one of these wings is a large kitchen thirty feet high, with an open cupola on the top: near it are a larder, brewhouse, and laundry, with rooms over them for servants; the upper sort of servants are lodged in the older wing, which has also here wardrobes and a storeroom for fruit. On the top of all, a leaden cistern, holding fifty tons of water, driven up by an engine from the Thames, supplies all the waterworks in the courts and gardens, which lie quite round the house, and through one of which a grass walk conducts to the stables, built round a court, with six coach-houses and forty stalls.

FIG. 98.—Trap-ball

"To the gardens we go down from the house by seven steps, into a gravel walk that reaches across the garden, with a covered arbour at each end of it. Another, of thirty feet broad, leads from the front of the house, and lies between two groves of tall lime trees, planted in several equal ranks, upon a carpet of grass: the outsides of these groves are bordered with tubs of bays and orange trees. At the end of this broad

Fig. 99.—The Great Room at Kenwood, Highgate, N. London
Designed by Robert Adam in 1767

Sixteenth-Century Hall, Fig. 28.   Seventeenth-Century Saloon, Pl. 22

walk, you go up to a terrace four hundred paces long, with
a large semicircle in the middle, from whence are beheld the
queen's two parks, and a great part of Surrey: then going
down a few steps, you walk on the banks of a canal six hundred
yards long and seventeen broad, with two rows of limes on
each side of it.

"On one side of this terrace a wall, covered with roses and
jessamines, is made low, to admit the view of a meadow, full
of cattle; and at each end a descent into parterres, with fountains and waterworks. From the biggest of these parterres we
pass into a little square garden, that has a fountain in the
middle, and two greenhouses on the sides, with a convenient
bathing apartment in one of them, and near another part of
it lies a flower garden. Below all this, a kitchen garden, full
of the best sorts of fruits, has several walks in it fit for the
coldest weather."

So far as the inside of the house was concerned, the entrance
court led into "a large hall, . . . the walls of it covered with
a set of pictures done in the school of Raphael. Out of this,
on the right hand, we go into a parlour, thirty-three feet by
thirty-nine. . . . From hence we pass, through a suite of
large rooms, into a bedchamber of thirty-four feet by twenty-
seven; within it a large closet, that opens into a greenhouse.
On the left hand of the hall . . . we go up eight-and-forty
steps, ten feet broad. . . . The roof of this staircase, which
is fifty-five feet from the ground, is forty feet by thirty-six,
and filled with the figures of gods and goddesses. . . . From a
wide landing-place on the stair's-head, a great double door
opens into an apartment of the same dimensions with that
below, only three feet higher. . . ." The saloon on this floor
was 35 feet high, 36 feet broad, and 45 feet long, and you could
have put the whole of a moderate-sized modern house into
this one room. We need not continue the description further
to give an idea of how palatial some of these eighteenth-
century houses were.

Our illustration, Fig. 99, is of the great room at Kenwood,
designed by Robert Adam in 1767 for Lord Mansfield. The
house, which is open to the public, is well worth a visit.
The columns shown in the foreground have "Corinthian"

caps, and a very beautiful effect is obtained by placing these
in the open, and taking the entablature over it across the
front of the apsidal
semicircular recesses
at the ends of the
hall. The apses are
finished with half-
domed ceilings,
which pick up the
same line as the cir-
cular vault over the
main body of the
hall. This vault is
beautifully decora-
ted, and the panels
filled with paintings.
Altogether a very
appropriate back-
ground for the fine
ladies and gentlemen
shown in the picture.
Before leaving this
drawing, we should
like to point out that
the architectural de-
tail is daintier and
more graceful than
the work of the first
half of the century,
also in the orna-
ment, by the employ-
ment of the "honey-
suckle" design, there
is an early indication

Founded on Barrow Hall, Essex

FIG. 100.—Staircase, late Eighteenth Century
Sixteenth-Century Staircase, Fig. 26
Seventeenth-Century Staircase, Fig. 59

of the Greek Revival. This followed on the publication, in
1762, by Stuart and Revett of their book on the *Antiquities
of Athens*, and the spirit of change was in the air. At the end
of George II's reign, Horace Walpole started building
Strawberry Hill, Twickenham, in the "Gothic" manner,

and "Greek" and "Gothic" were destined in the end to triumph over "Palladian."

The next illustration, Fig. 100, is of a staircase, and has been selected because it shows, like the first one illustrated in Vol. I, Chapter I, a circular treatment, though the centre stone newel in this case is missing. As well, the balustrade is in iron. Sir Christopher Wren did a very beautiful circular staircase at St. Paul's Cathedral. The steps were solid blocks of stone, with a moulded nosing worked on the front edge, and returned at the ends, and the steps, cut radiating to the centre, were built into the wall at one end, so that each step becomes a cantilever, the front edge of one resting on the back edge of the next below. A very beautiful and structurally sound method of construction. All sorts of designs were used in connection with the iron balustrade. The King's Staircase at Hampton Court is the work of the great smith Jean Tijou (p. 129), who was employed by Wren, and the treatment consists of panels filled in with scrolls and foliage, which repeat up the staircase, but the junction between the panels is not very noticeable, and the effect that of a continuous pattern of splendid wrought iron work. Later the balustrade became a succession of single balusters, and the favourite patterns for these were based on a lyre, or were S-shaped. The former have been shown on the drawing, and are alternated with plain bars, the handrail being in mahogany. By the way, we should explain that the eighteenth-century small boy under the stairs is not weeping, but hiding from his sister, and has been drawn like this, because we know of another to-day who considered that he was rendered invisible in this way.

We have spoken of the great houses and of the beautiful interior decoration of the eighteenth century, and we will now look at the furniture that filled the rooms of these houses. Toward the end of the seventeenth century oak gave place to other woods. Painted beech was used and walnut. The Portuguese leather-back chair of the reign of Charles II made in compliment to his wife, Catherine of Braganza, was altered to furniture, the design of which was governed by the strong Dutch influence of the reign of William of Orange and Mary. In the time of homely Queen Anne walnut was the favourite

wood and furniture
began to lose its pon-
derous proportions
and to take on a line
more conducive to
comfort. Mahogany
was regarded as a
luxury, although it is
believed that there is
at least one set of
chairs of this wood
still in existence which
was made in the year
1715.

One interesting
point is that whereas
until the eighteenth
century, furniture was
merely designated as
belonging to some
period, from now
on, design became a
question of individu-

FIG. 101.—Chippendale Chair, 1750

ality and not of periods only. Furniture was now divided
into schools of design, and given the name of the creator of

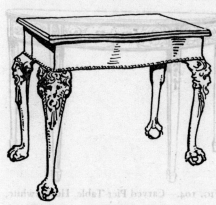

FIG. 102.—Carved Side Table, 1735

that style. Hence we
get the three great
names of Chippendale,
Hepplewhite, and
Sheraton. Chippendale
was the first great
designer of furniture
in the eighteenth
century. He and his
school held sway from
1750 until 1780. The
chair of 1750, Fig. 101,
is made in mahogany
and is a good example

FIG. 103.—Hepplewhite Shield-back Chair, 1775

of Chippendale's type of work. The decoration is founded on the acanthus leaf. The table, Fig. 102, made a little earlier, about 1735, is in walnut, has masks carved on the knees of the legs, and ball and claw feet. It is generally supposed that the ball and claw feet are an adaptation from the Oriental design of a dragon's claw clasping a pearl. Chippendale's genius was such that he took many and apparently incongruous motifs and welded them into one harmonious design.

While speaking of furniture, we must not leave out the hangings, and the embroidery which is still an art at which the modern woman may well marvel. There existed also the great tapestry factory at Mortlake, which produced cushions and bed hangings and daybeds of tapestry similar to those of Gobelins.

Many books of furniture were brought out, with engraved plates of the designs of furniture-makers, famous or less well known to the general public.

Kent of course is well known, but

FIG. 104.—Carved Pier-Table, Hepplewhite, 1775

there were also Manwaring, Ince, Mayhew, Johnson, and others.

Hepplewhite, who practised from 1775 until 1795, evolved a more delicate type of furniture; he used inlay, both in pattern and line in various woods, and his furniture is less solid and more elegant than that of his predecessor and rival. He was influenced by the Adam brothers and effected a more

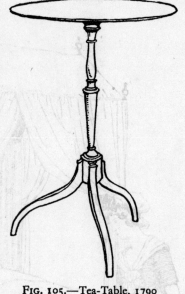

FIG. 105.—Tea-Table, 1790

FIG. 106.—Cane-back Chair, with painted Panels, 1800

classical line than Chippendale. Fig. 103, made in 1775, is of mahogany inlaid with boxwood; the shield-shaped back is very typical of this school. The table, Fig. 104, of 1775 is a pier-table of mahogany, very delicately carved in low relief, but this is an exceptional piece, in that it is carved and not inlaid. In general the pattern and colour was achieved by inlay and

FIG. 107.—A Tent Bed

Sixteenth-Century Bed, Fig. 27.   Seventeenth-Century Bed, Fig. 60

many woods were used such as tulipwood, walnut, sycamore, boxwood, satinwood, rosewood, pear, and others.

Sheraton, whose influence was active from 1790 until 1805, though certainly great in his earlier, more restrained, and classical work, marks the decline and fall of the art of furniture design; his last efforts, strange and often bizarre, tell of the decay of a great mind, and from 1805 onward we resign ourselves bit by bit to the horrors of the mahogany Victorian era.

The little table, Fig. 105, of the year 1790 is of mahogany and is one of the new little "tea-tables" then so fashionable in the polite world. It has a grace and charm, a little frail perhaps, all of its own, and the chair also, Fig. 106, of 1800 still has charm. It is of painted beech with cane back and seat and little painted pictures as ornament, and influenced by the prevalent fashion for everything classic, it still retains a feeling of symmetry which is pleasing to the eye.

Our next illustration, Fig. 107, is of a tent bed, so called for the very obvious reason that its shape suggested a tent. Such beds were, of course, considerably cheaper than those made of mahogany, with elaborately turned, fluted, and carved posts and tester. These latter followed on the lines of the sixteenth-century bed, illustrated in Fig. 27, but were lighter and more graceful in detail. With the tent bed it was only necessary to have a light iron framework to support the hangings, and little brass finials showing above the latter. There is a bed of this type at the Victoria and Albert Museum, South Kensington, which formerly belonged to David Garrick, the eighteenth-century actor, but, generally speaking, they were found in the less important houses. These beds were used well on into the nineteenth century, and perhaps their framework of iron suggested the very terrible brass-bound iron bedsteads of Victorian times. A tent bed is shown

FIG. 108.—Boy with Parachute

in one of the illustrations to *Dame Wiggins of Lee and her Seven Wonderful Cats*. This was published in 1823, and its illustrations are very interesting for their details of cottage interiors. Messrs. George Allen & Unwin publish reprints of this amusing book. Here is one of the verses:

> "While she ran to the field
> To look for its dam,
> They were warming the bed
> For the poor sick lamb:
> They turn'd up the clothes
> All as neat as could be;
> 'I shall ne'er want a nurse,'
> Said Dame Wiggins of Lee."

Five of the cats are shown airing the sheets with a warming-pan; one is assisting the "poor sick lamb" into the tent bed, and the other is holding the night-cap, which everybody wore.

Writing of furniture gives us the opportunity to illustrate an early piano, Fig. 109, dating from the end of the eighteenth century. This finishes the sequence of drawings commencing with the harp.

Pianos were invented in 1709 by a Florentine, and the distinctive difference between them and harpsichords and virginals is that the strings are struck by little hammers in the former, and in the latter plucked. The harpsichord, as its name would suggest, and in the way it was operated, was nearer of kin to the harp than the piano, but they are all related.

The keyboard of the early piano consisted of balanced levers, which, struck at one end by the finger, raised at the other a contrivance called the damper. This damper could be kept up as well by another lever, which had a corresponding effect to putting on the loud pedal in a modern piano. The keyboard lever had another lifter on it, which struck up against the undersides of the strings little hammers, hinged at one end, and hanging down underneath. Boys and girls who are interested in music should go to South Kensington, where, by applying at the office, they will be shown the working parts of the exhibits. It will make their playing more interesting

PLATE 39

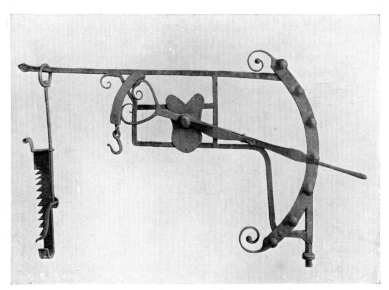

The Every Collection, Lewes

Elaborate Pot-crane, with small Crane attached

Painting by W. B. Bigg, R.A., 1783

A Cottage Interior with old Woman getting her Tea

PLATE 40

Engraving by H. Fletcher from a Drawing by J. Nichols

Stalls in the old Stocks Market, 1738, on the Site of
the Mansion House

Engraving after J. Wright of Derby

An Iron Foundry, *c.* 1780

FIG. 109.—Piano (end of Eighteenth Century)

Clavicytherium, Fig. 30.   Spinet, Fig. 62

to them, when they realise how much patient and very beautiful
work has been done to make it possible. The Museum has
some splendid examples of different sorts of instruments.

Antonio Stradivari made his best violins in this century,
between 1700–25, and Giuseppe Guarneri was his rival.

Figs. 110, 111 give the music of "Under the Greenwood
Tree," by Thomas Arne (1710–1778), which is Mr. Milne's
selection for the eighteenth century.

We can now leave music and write about cooking. Pl. 38
shows the sort of fireplace which was common to farmhouse
kitchens and cottages for several centuries. With plenty of
width, sufficient depth was arranged to give seats on each
side, and across the opening in front ran a sturdy oak beam,
often with a little curtain underneath it. Sometimes at the side
of the seats little cupboards were arranged, where pipes and
tobacco could be kept, and a bottle of spirits on which duty
had not been paid; if the exciseman was a friend, and the

187

FIG. 110.—First half of "Under the Greenwood Tree"
Sixteenth-Century Song, Fig. 31.   Seventeenth-Century Song, Fig. 63

Fig. 111.—Second half of "Under the Greenwood Tree"

night cold, he asked no questions. Small recesses in the brick-work were formed, where tinder and matches could be found. The tinder was made by putting woollen or cotton rags into the fire, which, when well alight, were placed in the bottom of the tinder-box and covered with the damper, which was a sheet of metal fitting down into the box. The steel was a piece of metal bent round and held in the left hand, and struck with a piece of flint until a spark dropped on to the tinder. The spark was blown up, and then the match lighted from the glow. The match was a thin strip of wood dipped into brim-stone. Lucifer matches did not come until well on in the nineteenth century.

The wood fire, though, seldom went out from one year's end to the other, and when the farmer came down very early in the morning, he raked the ashes until he found some still glowing, and then put on dry faggots and blew up the fire with the bellows. The ashes were not cleared away because these gave the heart to the fire. The outer edges were capital places to cook potatoes in, or broil mushrooms in their skins turned cup uppermost. Saucepans had small iron trivets, or stands, so that they could be pushed into the hot ashes. Pots were suspended over the fire from wrought iron cranes, as shown in the photo (Pl. 38). This example is from Sussex, and shows how the crane can be swung horizontally and the pot moved up and down by the lever which fits into the projecting knobs on the curved strip at the back. Practical fellows, these old smiths. In cottages a simpler ratchet arrange-ment was used. An iron rod, suspended from a bar in the chimney, had a loose clip at the bottom end. This clip fitted over the saw-like teeth of a flat piece of metal, which at its upper end was arranged to work up and down on the iron rod by a ring; at its lower end was the hook for the pot, the height of which could be adjusted by the clip and the ratchet. One of these is shown fitted loose on the end of the crane shown in Pl. 38, and we illustrate the same type with "idle-back" attachment in Vol. III, Fig. 24. A typical cottage fireplace with a bake oven on the left is also seen in Pl. 38, which is worth a close look for all the fittings of the interior.

The fire-dogs had hooks on the front, in which were placed the long spits, reaching across the front of the fire from dog to dog. The joint or fowl to be roasted was trussed on to the spit, which in the case of the bird passed right through it. In the case of a large joint a cradle spit was used. In this form the main spit was divided into an oblong frame in the centre, at the ends of which were spindles with screw-threads worked on to them. This enabled two oblong hoops, with an eyelet hole at each end, to be placed over the spindles, and turned with a thumb-screw down on to the joint, which was thus securely held. Or the spit had a forked prong which moved on it, and after being stuck into the joint could be screwed up tight. The spits had a pulley wheel at one end, from which lines were taken, like belting in a factory, to some such mechanical arrangement as was shown in Fig. 65, or they were worked by a smoke-jack in the chimney over. This consisted of a vane which was turned by the upward current of hot air and smoke, and so supplied the power. In Vol. III, Fig. 30, is seen a turnspit from a Welsh inn kitchen, worked by a dog. Fire-dogs are also called andirons, brand-irons, and brand-dogs; sometimes the tops of the standard were made cup-shaped, so that spiced ale might be kept warm.

When the spits were not in use, they were kept on a spit rack over the mantel-shelf outside; this latter came just above the beam across the opening, and held the "Toby" jugs, brass candlesticks, and other treasures of the housewife.

An iron fire-back came behind the fire, and was often very beautifully decorated with heraldic emblems. The bacon was placed in a smoke chamber formed in the flue over the fire, and so arranged that the bacon could be put in from a staircase, or upper floor, at the side of the chimney. Gilbert White, writing to his friend Pennant in 1771, said: "There is a small long shining fly in these parts, very troublesome to the housewife, by getting into the chimneys, and laying its eggs in the bacon while it is drying."

Fig. 112, of the toasting dog, makes us think of the rude term "hot dog." The dog must have been very hot when the sausage was cooked; however, made of wood, and about the same size as a fox terrier, he is a gay little fellow.

FIG. 112.—A Toasting Dog from a house in Suffolk

Please note how obligingly his tail has been turned into a handle.

Gilbert White wrote the *Natural History of Selborne*. This book grew out of a series of letters which, started in 1767, were addressed to two of his friends—Thomas Pennant, a Welsh naturalist, and Daines Barrington, interested in the same pursuit. These letters were not at first intended for publication, but they proved so interesting, that White's correspondents suggested that they should be brought out in book form, and this was done in 1789. It is very interesting that this book, which is valuable from the scientific point of view, appeals to us, as Pepys' diary does, because of the acute observation which enables us to realise a little part of the past. Gilbert White, Fellow of Oriel, little thought when he was sitting in his garden at Selborne, watching the birds, and then writing to his friends of their ways, that the letters would become a book, and as such be famous. He must have been a charming old man, and perhaps Austin Dobson had him in mind when he wrote:

> "He lived in that past Georgian day,
>   When men were less inclined to say
> That 'Time is Gold,' and overlay
>   With toil their pleasure;
> He held some land, and dwelt thereon,—
>   Where, I forget,—the house is gone;
> His Christian name, I think, was John,—
>   His surname, Leisure."

One of White's letters to Barrington, written on November 1, 1775, is about "the use of rushes instead of candles," and is of interest to us in these days of gas and electricity. We are told that the common soft rush was used and gathered in the summer and autumn. "As soon as they are cut they must be flung into water and kept there, for otherwise they will dry and shrink, and the peel will not run. At first a person would find it no easy matter to divest a rush of its peel or rind, so as to leave one regular, narrow, even rib from top to bottom that may support the pith." . . . "When these *junci* are thus prepared they must lie out on the grass to be bleached and take the dew for some nights, and afterwards be dried in the sun. Some address is required in dipping these rushes in scalding fat or grease. . . . The careful wife of an industrious Hampshire labourer obtains all her fat for nothing; for she saves the scummings of her bacon-pot for this use: and, if the grease abounds with salt, she causes the salt to precipitate to the bottom by setting the scummings in a warm oven." We are told that a good rush, 2 feet $4\frac{1}{2}$ inches long, "burnt only three minutes short of an hour, and gave a good clear light," but "watch lights (coated with tallow), it is true, shed a dismal one, but then the wick of these have two ribs of the rind, or peel, to support the pith, while the wick of the dipped rush has but one. The two ribs are intended to impede the progress of the flame and make the candle last."

White gives some interesting calculations. 1600 rushes = 1 lb. in weight. Assuming each rush burnt only half an hour, a poor man obtained 800 hours' light for 3s. This was based on 1 lb. of rushes using up 6 lb. of grease in dipping, and if the rushes were bought they cost 1s. a lb. and the grease 4d. per lb. A working-class family used about $1\frac{1}{2}$ lb. of rushes, or 2400 lights, in the year. White wrote: "Little farmers use rushes much in the short days, both morning and evening, in the dairy and kitchen," and Fig. 113 shows the rush-light holder in which they were used.

There is an interesting note in the *Natural History* showing that metheglin, which was a fermented liquor made from honey, was being made in 1775. "When metheglin was making he would linger round the tubs and vessels, begging a draught of what he called bee-wine."

Now we can leave houses and housekeeping for a little, and go into the gardens. Fig. 114 shows a garden house at the end of George I's reign, which is an amusing little hexagonal structure. Our readers must be getting quite used to plans, so will not need to be told that this is what the small decorative spot is, shown at the lower left-hand corner. It has been taken at the level of the seats, and illustrates the clever way these have been arranged. The right-hand plan shows the circular dome imposed on the hexagonal cornice. Any boy

FIG. 113.—Rush-light Holder

or girl who is so inclined, might try the effect of an octagonal treatment. It is great fun experimenting with geometrical figures, and those who are architecturally minded should study the steeples to Wren's City churches, and see how he worked up from perhaps a square base, through all sorts of shapes, to a circular dome. It is these large shapes, and the structure of the building, which settle its architectural character and success, rather than the mouldings and carving, which are only trimmings.

Founded on a Temple in the garden of The Moot, Downton, Wilts

FIG. 114.—Garden House (end of George 1's Reign)

A pleasant feature of this garden house is the plaster vault
springing out from over the seats to just behind the architrave
of the entablature. The columns under the latter are of the

195

"Doric" order. On the frieze of the entablature are shown small projections with vertical sinkings; these are called triglyphs, the space between is the metope, and in the old classical buildings these spaces were often decorated with ox skulls carved in relief.

Gardens until about this time, continued to be designed in the formal lines described on page 39. There were fine avenues of trees, fish-ponds and bowling-greens, clipped yew hedges and topiary work, terraces and flights of steps, enlivened with beautiful stone and lead vases and garden sculpture. Then a sad change came about in the middle and end of the century, as a reaction from the formalism of the older gardens, which people began to find dull. Addison wrote in the *Spectator* that he disliked "trees rising in cones, globes, and pyramids," and that "he would rather look upon a tree in all its luxuriancy and diffusion of boughs and branches." William Kent, the architect, laid out gardens, and as he worked on the principle of "Nature abhors a straight line," it can easily be understood that the old formal gardens did not appeal to him. He tried to make his gardens as natural in appearance as possible, and even went to the length of planting occasional dead trees "to give the greater air of truth to the scene"—a very hideous mockery.

Lancelot Brown, *b.* 1715, was a pupil of Kent, and followed his malpractices. He it was who was nicknamed "Capability" Brown, because he was fond of talking of the capabilities of any jolly old garden that he was called in to improve and destroy, and this he did in so ruthless a fashion that very few remain to show us what they were like. He destroyed the gardens at Buckingham House described on page 176, but was a very successful man, becoming the Royal Gardener at Hampton Court, where he planted the celebrated vine in 1769.

Sir William Chambers, another architect, published a book on *Oriental Gardening* in 1772, and he designed the pagoda at Kew in the fashionable Chinese manner. His work in this style was always restrained and kept within limits. Other men, without his knowledge, produced some amazing freaks, but the little Temple of Æolus at Kew, also designed by

Chambers, and not Chinese, is far more interesting and a quite beautiful little building.

Chambers hoped to infuse a little more interest into garden design, and complained in his book that "our gardens differ very little from common fields, so closely is common nature copied in most of them. There is generally so little variety in the objects, such a poverty of imagination in the contrivance, and of art in the arrangement, that these compositions rather appear the offspring of chance than design, and a stranger is often at a loss to know whether he is walking in a meadow or in a pleasure-ground, made and kept at a considerable expense."

Country houses and gardens suggest the coaches which were necessary to reach them from town, and as the centuries progress, we find that people became less contented with staying at home all the year round, and began to expect a holiday away. Fashionable folk went to stay at Tunbridge Wells, Epsom, Bath, and Cheltenham. Sea-bathing became popular, and there is a print of Scarborough sands in 1735, showing quite a nice bathing-machine, and people swimming in the sea. Later on, Margate, Brighton, and Weymouth became fashionable.

The subject of travel is one of considerable interest. Saddle-horses seem to have been the first method, and, like the pack-horses used for carrying goods, could pick their way over narrow and rough roads. Parties of people on foot often accompanied the pack-horses for the safety afforded by numbers. At the end of the sixteenth century, large broad-wheeled waggons travelled between towns with goods and passengers, and were called stages. Hackney coaches began about 1605, and stage coaches about 1640, the latter being like large private coaches. Outside passengers sat in a basket between the hind wheels, or sat on the roof, as shown by Hogarth in a picture painted in 1730. Mail coaches were started towards the end of the eighteenth century, and letters before this were delivered by the post-boys, who took the private coaches by stages. Gloucester was a day's journey from London, and Hereford $1\frac{1}{2}$ days. In the nineteenth century we used steam on railways, and the twentieth is destined to take to the air. There were amusing disputes in the eighteenth

FIG. 115.—Post-Chaise

Sixteenth-Century Coach, Fig. 40. Seventeenth-Century Vehicles, Fig. 66, Pl. 26.
Eighteenth-Century Vehicles, Figs. 115-119

century about road-making. Laws were passed to try and make the stage waggons have very wide wheels, to assist in rolling the roads, but the owners very much objected to this. Roads were made by the parishes, who charged tolls to those using them.

Mr. Felton, an eighteenth-century coach-builder, wrote in 1790: "Carriages should always be built adapted to the places for which they are destined, whether for town, country, or the Continent; as a greater stress is laid upon the carriages in drawing over stones than on a smooth road. This makes it absolutely necessary to build stronger for the town than if intended for the country only, owing to the general goodness of our English roads; it is also necessary to build stronger for the Continent than even for the town, as the badness of their roads obliges them to use six horses where we should use two." This means that the roads in towns were paved with granite cobbles, which would shake the framework of a carriage badly. In the seventeenth and early eighteenth centuries there were not any pavements, but foot passengers were protected by lines of posts along the side walks, as can be seen in the views of Loggan, or Hogarth. Later in the eighteenth century pavements as we now have them came into use.

The illustration, Fig. 115, shows a post-chaise, or a chaise

FIG. 116.—Perch Phaeton, 1790

Sixteenth-Century Coach, Fig. 40. Seventeenth-Century Coach, Fig. 67, Pl. 26.
Eighteenth-Century Vehicles, Figs. 115–119

in which one posted from town to town, hiring the horses
at the posting houses. It has a straight perch, rather like the
timber waggon in Fig. 66, only the place of the standards has
now been taken by upright springs from the ends of which
the chariot-shaped body is suspended by leather braces, with
additional straps over for steadying purposes. Luggage was
carried on the front transom and back axle-tree, and on the
roof as well.

Fig. 116 is of a perch phaeton of 1790, and this was the
sporting conveyance of the time; the fact that it was undoubtedly dangerous probably added a zest to its use. There
are double perches of a graceful swan-neck pattern. The body
is attached to upright springs in front, and suspended by
leather braces from others at the back, with additional straps
to prevent swaying. Luggage is carried fore and aft.

Fig. 117 shows a gig, and again the body is suspended from
curved springs by leather braces; when the body was fixed
in the shafts, with long horizontal springs under attached to
the axle-trees, it became a whisky. A one-horse phaeton was
like a gig on four wheels; a curricle, a gig drawn by two horses;
a cabriolet, a gig with a hood.

FIG. 117.—Gig

Sixteenth-Century Coach, Fig. 39. Seventeenth-Century Vehicles, Fig. 66, Pl. 32.
Eighteenth-Century Vehicles, Figs. 117–119

Landaus were first made in 1757, at the town of that name
in Germany; like a coach, the upper part was made to open
in halves, and fall back at an angle. Landaulets were chariots
made to open. Sulkies contained only one person, and by the
French were called *Anglaises désobligeantes*.

Fig. 118 shows an old waggon from Kent, the main interest
of which is in the shape of the body. Nowadays the waggon

FIG. 118.—An Old Waggon

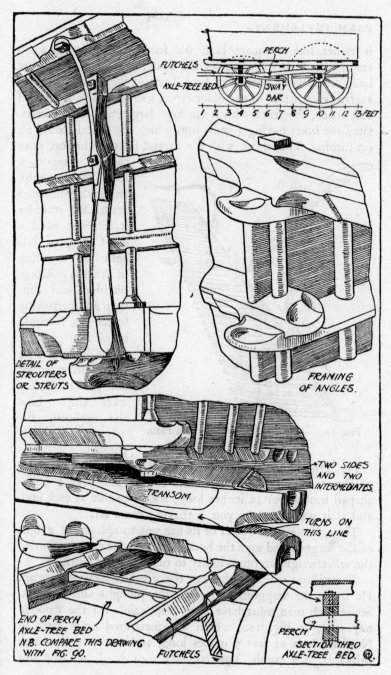

FIG. 119.—Details of an old Waggon found at Tring, Hertfordshire

is rather like a square box, the front wheels being small enough to turn round under the body, but small wheels are bad for drawing over farm land, because the smaller bearing surface cuts in; so in the older types, used for farm work and soft roads, the front wheels are kept larger, and this necessitated the body having a waist into which the wheels could go on turning. This waist, with the curved lines of the top, gave the old waggons a look of the ship, and as they bumped across the stubbles it did not need a great deal of imagination to think of them as galleons, pitching and dipping and curtseying to the sea. It would be nice to go back to the days when we played in waggons and pretended they were ships. Like the galleon, the waggon was gaily painted.

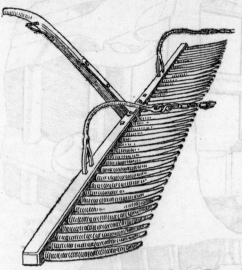

FIG. 120.—Wooden Hay Rake from a Farm in Norfolk

Fig. 119 gives some details of an old waggon, and examples of the work done with the draw-shave. This was a knife-shaped tool, about 12 inches long, with a handle at each end, and as it was drawn to you, a shaving came off.

Though the main object of its use was to reduce the weight of the waggon and save the horses, at the same time it afforded the wheelwright an opportunity to ornament his work.

The village wheelwright was the great country craftsman. He made the waggons and carts, the ploughs and harrows. Some such man must have been responsible for the wooden hay rake, as Fig. 120, which we discovered on a farm in Norfolk. It is 11 feet 9 inches long, and made on the same principle as a comb. You combed your head, so why not comb your fields! It was pulled by a horse, and when sufficient hay or corn had been collected, the horse was stopped and backed, and the rake pulled back by the small iron handle at the side of the wooden one. This latter was then pushed down so that the rake rode over the collected hay when the horse was restarted.

All should read *The Wheelwright's Shop*, by George Sturt, published in 1923. Mr. Sturt was a working wheelwright, and his book a delightful one. A sister book was issued in 1937 on *The Village Carpenter* by Walter Rose of Haddenham, Bucks.

As men became more travelled, they seem to have felt the need of common meeting-places, where they could see their friends and discuss the news of the day. We have mentioned the Mermaid Tavern, where Shakespeare and Jonson indulged in wit combats. Old Pepys was a sociable sort of person, and liked to go to the coffee-houses, where, as he said, there was much "admirable discourse," and the custom was continued in the eighteenth century. Pl. 34 shows a lively scene in a coffee-house of the time of Queen Anne. Boswell's *Life of Johnson* has many accounts of such meetings, and though the Doctor was rather fond of putting Boswell in his place, yet the evenings appear to have been very happy occasions. Eighteenth-century London was, of course, a much smaller place than it is to-day, with not so many people in it, so the circle of one's acquaintance would seem larger and more friendly. It was during this period that the club developed out of the coffee-house, and so met the demand for a more aristocratic and exclusive meeting-place, where men of the same social standing could come together. These clubs were often run by individuals for their own profit, with a committee of members. Almack's was founded in 1764, and became Brooks's, 1778. Unlimited gambling took place there, and many notable men were members. Among others can be mentioned Charles James Fox, Pitt, Burke, Sir Joshua Reynolds, Garrick, Walpole, and Sheridan. Fig. 121 shows the gaming-room in an eighteenth-century club-house. Horace Walpole wrote of a gathering of gamesters: "They began by pulling off their embroidered clothes and put on frieze greatcoats, or turned their coats inside outwards for luck. They

Brooks's Club, London

FIG. 121.—A Gaming-Room

put on pieces of leather such as are worn by footmen when they clean knives to save their lace ruffles; and to guard their eyes from the light and to prevent tumbling their hair, they wore high-crowned hats with broad brims, and adorned with flowers and ribbons and masks to conceal their emotions, and each gamester had a small neat stand by him to hold a wooden bowl with an edge of ormolu to hold his rouleaux."

The gambling period in England seems to have extended from the reign of Anne to that of Victoria, and reached its height at the end of the eighteenth century, perhaps because the constant wars, and the change over to industrialism, unsettled men and introduced the spirit of wishing to snatch something from chance, instead of doing honest work. Hazard was the principal game played. Faro started in 1780, and was an adaptation of the Stuart game of basset. Whist, curiously enough, started in servants' halls, and at first had the undignified name of "Swobbers."

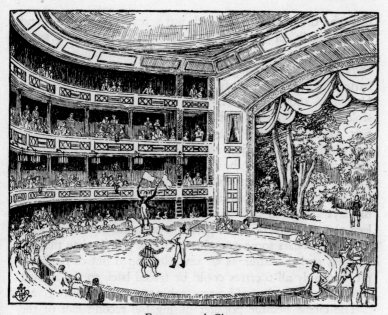

FIG. 122.—A Circus

Elizabethan "Plaic" House, Fig. 37.   Seventeenth-Century Theatre, Fig. 77

These notable men of the eighteenth century, winning and
losing fortunes, while Europe was in a state of ferment leading
up to the French Revolution, do not present a pleasant spectacle; so we turn with pleasure to more innocent amusements.
Our next illustration, Fig. 122, is of a circus, and here we
think that the fathers and mothers of our readers will recognise
an institution which was familiar in the days of their own
childhood, but is now not so often seen. That such should be
the case is rather a pity, the performances were so amusing.
First there was the circus; horses galloped round, and beautiful
ladies jumped through paper-covered hoops. The ring-master,
a superb if somewhat haughty individual, was in charge of
the proceedings, and the clown won all our young admiration
by the sallies of his wit. All kinds of other things happened,
but over all this part of the performance was cast a lovely
scent compounded of oranges and tan, horses and elephants,
which seemed like incense offered up to pleasure. Then

followed the pantomime, which was a real one, and Jack and the Beanstalk, or whatever it was, was recognisable as such, and not like a music-hall turn. There was a transformation scene, worthy, we thought, of Inigo Jones, and last came the harlequinade; our old friend the clown reappeared with Harlequin and Columbine, who was very lovely. Some one stole some sausages, and there was a policeman, and all this part was a delightful frolic to finish up with. To see how the romance of the ring still goes on you should read the fascinating account of the Circus in Mr. J. S. Clarke's *Circus Parade*, published in 1936 with many fine pictures.

The travelling circus is still with us, and occasionally displays are given in large buildings, but such performances lack the tradition of those given in a permanent circus. Our illustration bears some resemblance to the Elizabethan theatre, Fig. 37, and the latter, as we saw, developed out of the bear-pit. Probably all theatres could be traced back to the ancient arenas, where displays of horsemanship and combats were given.

The circus became popular during the second half of the eighteenth century. In the *Microcosm of London*, we are told that in the early days of George III's reign "a man excited the curiosity and called forth the wonder of the metropolis, by riding a single horse, on full gallop, while standing upright on the saddle. This person first exhibited in a field near Bancroft's almshouses, at Mile End; the place was enclosed with boards, to prevent any gratuitous view of the exercise, and the price of the admittance was one shilling." This individual was so successful that he retired, and set himself up in the principal inn in Derby on his savings.

Philip Astley started giving equestrian performances on a piece of ground in the Westminster Bridge Road in 1774, and here again the display was given in the open, behind boarded fences. Then the space was roughly covered in, and later a more permanent building which had been erected, was burned down. At the beginning of the nineteenth century, Philip's son built the one shown in our illustration, which was called Astley's Royal Ampitheatre. In the morning the circus was used as a riding-school, and it must be remembered that at this time everybody had to know how to ride.

As to the performances to be seen in the eighteenth-century circus, we do not think we can do better than to give an extract from an advertisement of 1780: "Part I will consist of the Lilliputian World, or Chinese Shadows: . . . Scene I.— A curious Opera Dancer, with all the new Attitudes, in a comic Dance called the Dutch Woman. Scene II.—The Dock Yard, with a Representation of the several Artists at work on a large Ship, to conclude with a Song on Admiral Rodney's Victory over the Spaniards, by Mr. Connel. Scene III.—The Lion Catchers [unfortunately no details are given of this]. Scene IV.—The Broken Ridge, with a Song by Mr. Wilkinson. Scene V.—The Duck Hunters. Scene VI.—The Storm, etc. The whole of the above Exhibition to conclude with a Horn-pipe, in a most extraordinary manner. Between the Acts of the Chinese Shadows will be presented an exhibition called the Theatre of Florence, representing several frontispieces of beautiful Fireworks, which have been displayed in different parts of Europe." Then followed "Horsemanship on a Single Horse—Tumbling and other agility of body—Horsemanship on two and three horses, in a manner truly entertaining— Slack Rope Vaulting on full swing in different attitudes— Polanders' tricks on Chairs, Ladders, etc.—The Clown on Horseback, with several parts of Horsemanship burlesqued— The Taylor riding on the Dancer, the Hunter, and Road Horse. The whole to conclude with the amazing performance of Men piled on Men, or the Egyptian Pyramids."

This is the sort of entertainment, then, that was provided for the Christmas holidays in the eighteenth century, and now we can pass to books and games.

Children's picture-books, of a kind within the reach of many, first came into existence in the eighteenth century. These were mostly little chap-books, illustrated with small woodcuts, sometimes gaily coloured, generally of the favourite nursery stories—Babes in the Wood, Mother Bunch, Dick Whittington, Cinderella, Red Riding Hood, the Sleeping Beauty, Bluebeard, Puss in Boots, and Little Tom Thumb; all old tales, some so old that their origin is lost in the mists of time.

The two pictorial alphabets: "A was an archer who shot

FIG. 123.—The Game of Bear-leader

Sixteenth-Century Game, Fig. 45. Seventeenth-Century Game, Fig. 78

at a frog," and "A was an apple-pie," were well known in the reign of Queen Anne. These books were usually bought of travelling pedlars called chapmen, or paultrie pedlars.

For the more restless spirits there were many games—battledore and shuttlecock, marbles, hot cockles, hunt the slipper, thread the needle, trap-ball (Fig. 98), and games with toy parachutes (Fig. 108) and peg-tops. Football is, of course, a very old game. It is spoken of in the fifteenth century, and in the reign of James 1 a rule was made to "debarre from this court all rough and violent exercise as the football, meeter for laming than for making able the users thereof." But boys still played the game, despite the rules of kings, and in Chester, Dorking, and elsewere it was always played in the streets on Shrove Tuesday.

In an eighteenth-century print, apprentices are to be seen playing football in the Strand. Bear-leader was a favourite game, and is the subject of the illustration, Fig. 123. It was played by several children, one blindfolded, who led another on his hands and knees by a cord. The blindfolded boy was the bear-leader, and it was his duty to prevent the others hitting the bear, who crouched beside him for protection.

Little girls had a game called "Queen Anne," which was played thus: the children stood in two lines which faced one another, one line hiding amongst themselves a ball. Both lines moved backwards and forwards reciting alternate lines of the following verses:

"Lady Queen Anne who sits in her stand [sedan chair]
And a pair of green gloves upon her hand,
As white as a lily, as fair as a swan,
The fairest lady in a' the land.

Come smell my lily, come smell my rose,
Which of my maidens do you choose?
I choose you one, and I choose you all,
And I pray Miss (——) yield up the ball.

The ball is mine and none of yours,
Go to the woods and gather flowers;
Cats and kittens bide within,
But all young ladies walk out and in."

The child who is named Queen Anne has the task of saying which child on the opposing side has the ball, and if she guesses right, the ball is given up to her with a curtsey.

One interesting thing to notice about children's toys is that there were until this time no regular toy-makers of the better-class toys, but each small object was made a replica in miniature of the full-size thing, by the regular craftsman to whom that particular trade belonged.

For instance, very charming little complete tea and dinner services were made by the great china makers of the day, and wonderful doll's furniture, by Sheraton and Chippendale themselves. Miniature kitchen sets were to be obtained, and for wealthy children the silversmiths made perfect models, in silver, of almost all the everyday things one can think of. Eighteenth-century dolls' houses are quite charming little Georgian houses, in miniature, true to style, and not, as now, without any sense of design at all.

Lead soldiers were cast, chiefly flat, and sometimes soldiers folded and painted on paper were seen; these were from 5½ to 7 inches high. Rocking-horses could be bought—

in fact, most of the toys that the child of to-day loves were beloved in the eighteenth century. Cheap mechanical toys, however, were not made until the end of the century, though we hear of peep-shows with dancing and musical figures in them. One wonderful mechanical and musical figure, 15 feet 6 inches high, called "The Flute Player," was made by a man named Vancouson, and was exhibited in Paris.

A grand marionette theatre was opened in St. James's Street by the poet Colley Cibber, and Smollett describes it as "the modish diversion of the time."

At Exeter Exchange, in the Strand, was a wild beast show, containing elephants, giraffes, lions, and tigers, and doubtless children were taken to see them, and enjoyed themselves, even as children do at the Zoo to-day. The eighteenth century was truly a great age for amusements of all kinds, and one very noticeable feature of the day was the number of spas, or tea-gardens, that sprang up. Their forerunner was the Spring Gardens at Whitehall, where Charles I played bowls and indulged in mild entertainments. Then came the Mulberry Gardens, spoken of by Pepys, where Dryden was seen eating tarts. It was closed in 1674. Islington Spa came into being in the early eighteenth century, being noted for its medicinal waters; the Princess Caroline and Amelia regularly took the waters there. Bagnigge Wells became of note for its many kinds of alfresco entertainments, also Marylebone Gardens, where fine singing was the attraction.

All these places in the early part of the century were simple and refined, and citizens of London could go there and take tea, listen to the music, and watch the varied flow of people promenading to and fro. In 1734 Peerless Pool (originally called Perilous Pool, and used for duck-hunting), situated where Old Street is now, was turned into an open-air swimming-bath: an artificial canal was also cut from it and stocked with fish, where those so inclined could fish for a small fee.

As time went on, the rivalry between the different gardens caused each to vie with the other in the luxuriousness and extravagance of their entertainments. Jenny's Whim, in Chelsea, had a bowling-green, a cockpit, and a pond where mechanical mermaids and fishes rose at intervals. There was a grotto where Harlequin and Mother Shipton started up when the visitor trod on a concealed spring. Unfortunately the character of these places gradually declined until it became necessary to put an end to the many scandals arising from them, and they were suppressed by law and finally disappeared.

In fashionable London the great rage from the reign of Queen Anne to that of George III was the giving of masked balls and assemblies. These were first organised as regular and public entertainments in 1708, by a Swiss named Heidegger, who was called by Henry Fielding "Surintendant des plaisirs d'Angleterre." They were scenes of extraordinary brilliance, and it was no uncommon thing for a dandy to change his costume three times in one evening. The Pantheon in Oxford Street was one of the favourite places for these assemblies, also Cornely's at Carlisle House, and Almack's. In fact, a regular set of people arose, who, taking a large house, made their living, often their fortune, by organising these masked entertainments, charging so much for each ticket of entrance.

The young dandies of Almack's, White's, and Boodle's (all exclusive gaming clubs) gave private masquerades at Carlisle House, and on one occasion 800 people were present, all in fancy dress, one lady as an Indian Sultana, having diamonds worth £100,000 on her head-dress. Mr. Garrick was there, we are told, as Bellarius. This was at the height of the rage for this form of amusement, but, like the tea-gardens, their popularity waned, many became disreputable, and they were gradually given up.

Let us now turn to another side of the picture, and see what attention was given to literature and scholarly learning. Booksellers' shops were still comparatively rare, and in Boswell's *Life of Johnson* we read that even in Birmingham only one was opened, and that on market day, by Johnson's father, Michael Johnson. But many great essayists and poets were rising, and in 1761 we hear that Sheridan delivered lectures on the English language in Edinburgh and at Bath. The first regular periodicals were published early in the eighteenth century. The *Tatler* commenced in 1709 and was followed by the *Spectator* in 1711, the *Guardian* and the *Rambler* in 1713, and the *Gentleman's Magazine* in 1731.

The first daily paper was printed permanently in 1702. It measured 14 by 8 inches. Some of these newspapers were arranged with one blank sheet, in order that Londoners could buy the paper, read it, and pass it on together with a note written by themselves on the blank sheet, to their friends in the country. All the best papers could be read at the coffee-houses for the fee of one penny.

In 1730 the original Methodists came into existence, and this name was first given to a society of students at Oxford who were noted for their earnest and methodical attention to devout exercises.

Certain charitable organisations were founded and in 1789 Hannah More and her sister Patty, with the financial assistance of Wilberforce, started the Cheddar Mission. She was then about 46 years old and spent most of her summers in a cottage she owned in a small village near Bristol. The district round the Cheddar Gorge was notorious for the savagery of its inhabitants, many of whom lived in caves in a completely uncivilised and wild state, all respectable country people giving the place a wide berth. Despite great opposition, Hannah More ventured, and, with infinite labour and in the face of many difficulties, succeeded in establishing schools and clubs, in reclaiming and civilising hundreds of women and children.

Another society also was formed, and was called in derision the "Blue Stockings." It was started by Mrs. Elizabeth Montague and her friends, women who met together for conversation only, without the usual adjunct of cards and frivolity. Certain clever men also came to Mrs. Montague's "salon," and Horace Walpole, Dr. Johnson, and Edmund Burke were frequent visitors, as were also Hannah More, Mrs. Thrale, and Frances Burney. Benjamin Stillingfleet, one of the shining lights in the society's discussions, was nevertheless eccentric in his dress, and it was the blue worsted stockings that he affected which caused the fashionable world to dub all the members just "blue stockings."

The manners of the eighteenth century were a curious mixture of coarseness and artificial elegance. Men could bow and posture, and turn a compliment gracefully, and yet use the most horrible oaths and enjoy the coarsest of pleasures, and great ladies too, although they could swoon and languish, would also swear and even spit, and often beat their maids cruelly. Table manners we should find somewhat coarse to-day. Swift mentions the appearance of "Doiley" napkins, so named from a leading linen draper who produced them, and in a book of table manners in 1703, the reader is counselled to wipe his knife on his napkin and not on his bread or on the tablecloth. Two-pronged forks were used; those with three prongs were still rare and expensive. As regards spoons, it mentions a basin being placed on the sideboard to wash them in, for, it says, "some (people) are so curious that they will not endure a spoon to be used in two several dishes." These books, however, were probably published for people who, having made money, wished to acquire gentility. Three o'clock was the usual dinner hour, and fashionable folk drank chocolate in their rooms in the morning. In the afternoon the fashionable world rode, drove or walked round Hyde Park and in the reign of Queen Anne rules were issued as to the keeping of it in proper order, lanterns were lit at nightfall on the road from Hyde Park to the Palace at Kensington, and we read that at this time lamps with thick convex glass began to be used in the streets of London which gave better light by far than the former lanterns. Even so the roads, not only in the country, but round and indeed in London, were unsafe at night. Bands of fashionable dissolute young men calling themselves Mohocks roamed the streets at night assaulting passers-by. Then came others called Scowerers, who broke up inns and meetings, always with a great noise. Others, too, called Nickers, broke windows after dark by the game of flicking pennies at them, and even in 1791 highway robberies were committed almost with impunity in all the roads leading out of London. Some of these roads were so unsafe that bands of armed horsemen were hired to ride with and protect coaches travelling on them. Piccadilly is spoken of as being "quite unsafe after dark," and in 1748 the French mail was robbed by highwaymen in Pall Mall at 8.30 p.m.

It was not until 1805 that the Bow Street horse patrol was

After Thomas Rowlandson, 1790

FIG. 124.—A Butcher's Shop

established by Sir Richard Ford. This consisted of thirteen parties of armed horsemen who patrolled the roads within a ten-mile radius of London, and gradually swept them clear of highwaymen and other "evilly disposed persons," and in 1829 Sir Robert Peel established policemen in London itself.

Shops were fewer then than now, and many goods were sold on barrows on the streets. Every trade had its own particular call, generally a singsong chant. Thread laces were called, also strawberries and all fruits, gingerbread toys and alphabets, eels, and chickens, and a host of other things, many to be seen in that charming series, *Tempest's Cryes of London*. One exhibition, started in 1761, which we have not yet mentioned, is spoken of in Boswell's *Life of Johnson* thus: "The artists have instituted a yearly exhibition of pictures and statues, in imitation, I am told, of foreign Academies. This year was the second exhibition. They please themselves much with the multitude of spectators, and imagine that the English school will rise in reputation. Reynolds is without a rival."

This exhibition is of interest. It was arranged by the Society of Artists, and held in the Adelphi; here Gainsborough first exhibited his work in London. Out of this was developed the Royal Academy of Arts, founded in 1768. Sir Joshua Reynolds was the first President, and Chambers the architect, Treasurer. Bartolozzi, Cosway, Angelica Kauffmann, and Benjamin West, were among the original members, and though Gainsborough does not figure in the list, his name is given as an R.A. in the first catalogue. Romney never became a member.

Reynolds once referred to Gainsborough as "our best landscape painter," but curiously enough the eighteenth-century folk did not buy his landscapes, and he was esteemed, like his rivals Reynolds and Romney, for his portraits. Gainsborough quarrelled with his fellow Academicians, but when he was dying of cancer, in 1788, sent for Reynolds, and almost his last words were addressed to him: "We are all going to heaven, and Vandyck is of the party." Boys and girls who are interested in painting should go to the National Gallery, and study the splendid examples of eighteenth-century painting they will find there.

Our tail-piece, Fig. 125, shows a typical piece of ornament, designed by Robert Adam, and as it happens to be the end-piece as well, we will doff our caps, wave brush and pen, and say "Good-bye" to our readers.

FIG. 125.—Eighteenth-Century Ornament

Sixteenth Century Ornament, p. 79.   Seventeenth Century Ornament, p. 146

INDEX

The references *in heavy type are to* the *figure numbers* of the text illustrations; the plates are indexed under "Pl."

INDEX

219